P9-DFC-457

The Right Questions

Truth, Meaning & Public Debate

Phillip E. Johnson

Foreword by Nancy Pearcey

InterVarsity Press
P.O. Box 1400, Downers Grove, IL 60515-1426
World Wide Web: www.ivpress.com
E-mail: mail@ivpress.com

©2002 by Phillip E. Johnson

All rights reserved. No part of this book may be reproduced in any form without written permission from
InterVarsity Press.

InterVarsity Press® is the book-publishing division of InterVarsity Christian Fellowship/USA®, a student
movement active on campus at hundreds of universities, colleges and schools of nursing in the United States of
America, and a member movement of the International Fellowship of Evangelical Students. For information
about local and regional activities, write Public Relations Dept., InterVarsity Christian Fellowship/USA, 6400
Schroeder Rd., P.O. Box 7895, Madison, WI 53707-7895, or visit the IVCF website at <www.ivcf.org>.

Scripture quotations, unless otherwise noted, are from the New Revised Standard Version of the Bible,
copyright 1989 by the Division of Christian Education of the National Council of the Churches of Christ in the
USA. Used by permission. All rights reserved.

ISBN 0-8308-2294-1

Printed in the United States of America ∞

Library of Congress Cataloging-in-Publication Data

Johnson, Phillip E., 1940-
   The right questions: truth, meaning and public debate/Phillip E.
Johnson
      p. cm.
   ISBN 0-8308-2294-1 (cloth: alk. paper)
   1. Apologetics. 2. Naturalism—Religious aspects—Christianity. I.
Title.
   BT1200 .J645 2002
   239—dc21   *2002006756*

P	18	17	16	15	14	13	12	11	10	9	8	7	6	5	4	3	2	1
Y	16	15	14	13	12	11	10	09	08	07	06	05	04	03	02			

Contents

Foreword by Nancy Pearcey. 7

Introduction: The Logical Train 27

1 Biology and Liberal Freedom. 31
THE HUMAN GENOME PROJECT AND THE MEANING OF LIFE
The Right Questions About Science, God and Morality

2 The Word of God in Education. 49
*The Right Questions About the Religious Foundations
of Education*

3 The First Catastrophe 79
UNARMED AMONG THE DRAGONS OF THE MIND
The Right Questions About Logic

4 My New Post 93
THE ROAD FORWARD
The Right Questions About the Meaning of Life

5 The Second Catastrophe 107
THE TOTTERING TOWERS OF FAITH
*The Right Questions About Religion and Tolerance
in a Pluralistic Society*

6 Genesis and Gender 127
The Right Questions About Genesis

7 Truth and Liberty 149
FREEDOM TO DISSENT AND FREEDOM TO DO RIGHT
The Right Question About Truth and Liberty

8 The Ultimate Question. 169
WHAT IS THE MOST IMPORTANT EVENT IN HUMAN HISTORY?

Foreword

The first time I contacted Phillip Johnson, he wasn't sure he wanted to talk to me. I had just read the manuscript of his first book, *Darwin on Trial*, and I was calling to request an interview.

The difficulty was, I was a contributing editor for the *Bible-Science Newsletter*, an unabashedly creationist publication (now defunct). As an adult convert to Christianity, Johnson was ready to question Darwinian materialism, but he wasn't sure he was ready to associate with outright creationists. He even consulted a friend over whether to grant the interview.

Fortunately, the friend was a close associate of mine as well, Charles Thaxton. (I had met Charlie in 1971 at L'Abri in Switzerland, where I heard him lecture on the flaws of evolution.) Thaxton encouraged him to go ahead with the interview, and thus began a personal friendship and professional association that have continued ever since.

In introducing this book I would like to cast a glance back over the past several years and describe the innovative ways Johnson has transformed the terms of the evolution debate. Having been involved in the debate for more than two decades (since 1977), writing on science and worldview issues, I can describe the lay of the land both before and since Johnson joined the fray. For those who have followed the evolution controversy for many years, this will explain what is new and significant in the Intelligent Design Movement. And for newcomers, it will be a helpful introduction to the current state of the debate.

Moreover, because this current book is the most personal of Johnson's published works, it seems appropriate to focus on the man himself and his influence. His innovative mode of operation can be instructive for Christians working in other areas as well, serving as a positive model for cultural engagement in any field or discipline.

Asking the Right Questions

Johnson's single most important contribution has been a keen sense of strategy. Christians trained in the sciences had done (and continue to do) excellent work in reviving and advancing standard critiques of evolutionary theory. But scientists are typically less adept at thinking strategically and mobilizing a movement.

The result was that theists across the spectrum fought each other instead of joining together to oppose the hegemony of materialistic evolution. I have vivid memories of acrimonious debates between various groups: young-earth creationists, old-earth creationists, flood geologists, progressive creationists, "gap" theorists and theistic evolutionists. They argued over the interpretation of terms in Genesis and the length of the creation "days." They argued over whether the Genesis flood explains the fossil record and how much "process" God employed in creating the world.

And as battling believers splintered into antagonistic groups, secularists were happy to fan the flames. As Johnson puts it, "They all but said, 'Let us hold your coats while you fight.' " Secularists had no need to work at marginalizing Christianity through a strategy of "divide and conquer" because Christians were doing all their work for them.

When Johnson entered the arena, he immediately launched a new strategy. Call it "unite and win." He rallied Christians behind the crucial point of confrontation with the secular world—the issue that stands at the heart of the conflict between Christianity and secular academia.

And what is that? It's the question of philosophical naturalism: Is nature all there is? Can natural forces alone explain the universe and everything in it? Did life arise by blind, materialistic, Darwinian processes, or does the evidence point to other forces? In confronting secular culture, these are the right questions to start with; all others are secondary. Christians may argue about the details of how God created or the timing of creation; but they all agree that the universe is the handiwork of a personal God. Likewise, on the other side, evolutionists may argue over the precise mechanism and timing of evolution—for example, whether natural selection needs to be supplemented by other mechanisms—but they agree that the overall process is blind, undirected, purposeless. Asking the right questions means bracketing peripheral issues in order to focus on the crucial point of whether the universe is an open or a closed system—and whether science therefore should be limited to naturalistic theories only or consider *any* theory that adequately explains the evidence, even one that invokes an intelligent agent.

In many ways, Johnson was applying the same principle in science that Francis Schaeffer had articulated in his cultural apologetics. One factor that made Schaeffer so effective was that he clarified the search for truth by sketching, in stark outline, what the basic choices are. When it comes to first principles, there are not really many viable options—indeed, only two. Either the universe is a closed system of cause and effect, or it is an open system. Either it is the product of impersonal, undirected natural forces, or it is the product of a personal agent. Every worldview has to start somewhere, Schaeffer used to say, and either we can start with time plus chance plus the impersonal, or we can begin with a personal being who thinks, wills and acts. As a student at L'Abri, I listened to one of his best-known lectures, "Possible Answers to the Basic Philosophical Questions," where he argues that if an impersonal beginning is inadequate to explain reality, then we have undercut a vast variety of philosophical systems without having to debate the myriad details that distinguish them.

In a similar way, Johnson cut through the conflicting claims of a vast variety of positions on origins by showing the crucial role played by initial philosophical commitments: Either nature is all that exists, and science is permitted to consider only naturalistic theories—in which case science is little more than applied naturalism—or there is something that transcends nature, and we must define science in terms that allow it to follow the evidence wherever it leads.

Uniting Christians Behind the "Big Ideas"

One of the beauties of Johnson's approach is that it has the potential to unite Christians across a broad spectrum. They might disagree over such details as the age of the universe, but all orthodox Christians can concur in rejecting a blind, mindless, materialistic mechanism for the origin and development of life. Johnson's approach is sometimes described as a middle ground or compromise position, but that's a misunderstanding. In fact, what he has proposed is not one more competing position at all; he has offered a logical analysis of the foundational ideas that unite *all* Christians, regardless of the details of their positions.

Having united on these defining principles, Christians may well discover a new spirit of unity and charity for taking up the old contentious issues once again. They can now treat the questions that once divided them as the subjects of friendly in-house debates. They can engage in amicable discussions over the interpretation of Genesis, the age of the universe, the range and limits of microevolution and common descent, and so on. Such lively debate is what science is all about.

Indeed, it's not too much to say that the Intelligent Design Movement has largely achieved this unity. It has become a "big tent" drawing together Christians across a wide range of disciplines and positions, from strict young-earth creationists to theistic evolutionists (at least those among the latter who acknowledge a role for divine direction). Along the way, the movement has picked up allies and cobelligerents among Jews, Muslims and even secularists who are willing to challenge the hegemony of naturalistic evolution.

Dividing the Opposition

The flip side of Johnson's strategy is to divide the opposition—and once again the starting question is the role played by philosophical naturalism.

Consider the definition of science itself. Most people hold an idealized image of science as impartial, unbiased empirical investigation. But in practice, Johnson argues, science has been co-opted into the camp of the philosophical naturalists and is often little more than applied naturalism. The effect is that the only theories considered acceptable are naturalistic ones.

Without this biased definition, Johnson argues, naturalistic evolution would not hold the privileged position it currently enjoys. If evolutionists are pressed for actual observable, empirical evidence in favor of their theory, inevitably they reach into the same grab bag and pull out the same examples of small-scale change, things like different breeds of dogs or variation in the size of finch beaks or radiation-induced mutations in fruit flies or the development of resistance to insecticide.

Exactly what do these changes amount to? They are small-scale adaptations that allow the organisms to survive under adverse conditions—in other words, minor adjustments that allow them to *stay* dogs or finches or fruit flies *or whatever they already are*. In no case do these minor variations demonstrate that the organism is changing into something new or that it originally evolved from something else. As Johnson has pointed out, the only reason people find such limited change convincing is that they have already been persuaded on *other* grounds—on philosophical grounds—that naturalism is true, or at least the only stance permissible within science. And once people have made that commitment, they can be impressed by relatively minor evidence.

Harvard biologist Richard Lewontin gave the game away in a highly revealing article in the *New York Review of Books* a few years ago—an article Johnson quotes frequently. Lewontin writes that science itself has been refashioned into a machine for cranking out strictly materialist theories. (In his words, science has been turned into "an apparatus of investigation and a set of concepts that produce material explanations.") The reason science has been so redefined, Lewontin writes, is "because we have a prior commitment, a commitment to materialism."

This stunning admission confirms what Johnson has long insisted: what drives the show is not the facts but the philosophy.

Yet it is certainly not the image of science cherished by most ordinary people, which is why Johnson's strategy is so devastating. His goal is to divide evolutionists according to these opposing definitions of science, to force out of the closet the doctrinaire ideologues—those who define science as a machine for churning out theories that fit their "prior commitment" to materialism—and set them apart from genuine scientists who are willing to follow the facts wherever they lead, regardless of the philosophical implications.

This crack in the scientific establishment is the target of what Johnson calls his "wedge strategy." By breaking open the ideologically closed scientific establishment, he hopes to create a new atmosphere of freedom, releasing science from the shackles of philosophical materialism.

Putting "Religion" Back on the Table

Johnson's innovative manner of framing the debate has been astonishingly effective in winning a respectful hearing in the secular world—certainly much more so than any previous attempts to challenge naturalistic evolution. One reason for his success is that his critique arises from within science itself instead of coming from outside.

In the nineteenth century, the Romantic movement arose as a reaction against the materialist, mechanistic science of the Enlightenment. Ever since, criticisms and protests have been raised from a variety of perspectives by artists, philosophers, theologians and others. Yet most scientists easily brushed these aside, because the arguments came from outside science, and for the modernist mindset, whatever falls outside science does not qualify as genuine knowledge.

Thus neither traditional creationism or theistic evolutionism made any significant inroads into the scientific establishment. Creationism began by asking, How do the teachings of the Bible relate to science? This is a perfectly valid question, just as believers should also ask how the Bible relates to economics or politics or the arts. Yet it is not the way to craft a message that secularists will hear. Critics could easily characterize creationism as the bald assertion that "God did it—end of discussion." The appeal to the Bible was dismissed as a "science stopper"—something that ends investigation and undercuts science. Mainstream scientists could ignore even cogent and compelling critiques of evolutionary theory if the only alternative seemed to be a leap from science into theology.

Theistic evolutionists took a different tack—but yielded parallel results. They were content to let the secularists define scientific knowledge so long as theology was allowed to put its own spin on whatever science decreed to be true. They gave up the claim that God's existence makes any *scientific* difference and accepted the scientific theories proposed by materialists and atheists, asking only to propose a theological meaning behind it all—not detectable by scientific means, admittedly, but known by faith.

In such a case, however, what would this theological meaning amount to? Theology is no longer acknowledged as an independent source of knowledge; it is merely a spiritual spin on the otherwise materialistic account given by science. Since this approach does not threaten the ruling regime of materialistic science, the scientific establishment is generally willing to tolerate it as a harmless delusion for those who need that kind of crutch.

Thus in different ways both traditional creationism and theistic evolutionism were dismissed as "religious," which in secular circles is a term of abuse meaning myth and fantasy. What makes design theory new is that it does not start by asking what the Bible teaches; it starts by asking what can be known by scientific means: Can the identifying marks of design be detected empirically? And thus it reconnects Christian theology to the empirical world and restores its status as a claim to cognitive knowledge. Theology is no longer a matter of merely subjective "belief" but a genuine knowledge claim.

Developing a Positive Case for Design

With Christians tangled in endless arguments over Genesis 1, Johnson redirected the debate along fruitful lines by jumping over Genesis and focusing on John 1:1. "In the beginning was the Word"—the *Logos*—the Greek word for reason, intelligence, rationality, information. The great confrontation in science today is between those who say life can be explained without recourse to reason or intelligence, and those who say life embodies information—the Word—and must be explained as the product of an intelligent agent.

The most dramatic supporting evidence for intelligent design comes from the discovery of DNA. Molecular biology has revealed at the core of life a code, a language, a message. As a result, the origin of life has been recast as the origin of new, complex forms of information. How do we explain the sequence of symbols in a message—any message? The sequence of letters in a book is not random, nor does it follow a rule or law (i.e., it is not a regular, repeating pattern, like a macro on your computer). Instead, the sequence has a third kind of structure that scientists call "specified complexity"—which means a complex sequence that fits a preselected pattern.

Specified complexity can be identified by rigorous mathematical formulas (as William Dembski has shown in *The Design Inference*), which means scientists are now equipped to go beyond merely negative critiques of naturalistic evolution by identifying the positive marks of design. In all cases where we *know* the source of information, like books and computer programs and musical scores, that source is an intelligent agent. It is logical to conclude that the source of information in living things is likewise intelligent.

The analysis of information is not new with Johnson, of course. Important forerunners include A. E. Wilder-Smith in *The Natural Sciences Know Nothing of Evolution,* and Charles Thaxton and his coauthors in *The Mystery of Life's Origin* (not to mention the last chapter of my own book with Thaxton, *The Soul of Science*). But Johnson helped press the issue of information to the center of the debate, making it the touchstone for constructing a positive case for design.

Asking the Right Questions in Theology

Having established John 1:1 as the central point of contact between science and Scripture, in this current book Johnson tackles the sticky issue of the interpretation of Genesis. Once again, his strategy is to cut through conflicting claims over the details and focus on asking the right questions. With Genesis, the place to begin is the question of historicity: Do the early chapters of Genesis tell us about events that actually happened?

Genesis was one of the first sections of the Bible to fall beneath the axe of nineteenth-century higher criticism. Critics insist that the early chapters of Genesis are not history but myth—pious inventions. Thus before we examine the details of what Genesis teaches, we must first establish whether it contains any cognitive content at all.

"In the beginning God created the heavens and the earth." Is this true or false? For many people, even asking such a question amounts to a category mistake. Genesis is a religious document, they might reply—the implication being that religions are not true or false, they're about people's "values." Even sincere believers may feel uncomfortable applying stark categories of true and false to scriptural statements. They may readily agree that religion is personally important ("It gives meaning to my life"; "It is true for *me*"), but is it *objectively* true?

The problem is that many Christians have absorbed a naturalistic framework in practice even if not in belief. Among theistic evolutionists this is often done explicitly. Many reject *metaphysical* naturalism as an overall philosophy but embrace *methodological* naturalism as proper within science. They argue that Christians must play by the rules of science—and the rule is that only naturalistic theories need apply. Johnson tartly replies, "Why should we let the naturalists make the rules? Why should we accept the starting assumption that God has never acted in ways accessible to scientific investigation? Why not challenge the rules and insist that science follow the data wherever it leads?"

Once again we can trace parallels between Johnson's work and that of Francis Schaeffer, who used the image of two chairs. Sitting in the naturalist's "chair," we would see the world filtered through a certain lens; sitting in the supernaturalist's "chair," Christians see the world through a much different lens. We are aware of an unseen realm in addition to the seen realm.

In practice, however, Christians are not always consistent. They may be intellectually convinced of the Christian worldview yet practice their professions on the basis of a naturalistic worldview. This is exactly what happens when Christians accept methodological naturalism in science.

That's not all. When naturalism is accepted in science, its implications spread like a virus to other areas. For example, the assumption that humans are the products of naturalistic evolution leads inexorably to the conclusion that religion and ethics have evolved as well—that they are merely products of the human mind that appear when the nervous system has evolved to a certain level of complexity. In Johnson's punchy phrasing, the choice is simple: Either God created us, or we created God—that is, we created the *idea* of God out of some emotional need or personal experience.

Thus naturalism leads to what is often referred to as the fact-value dichotomy—the mentality that grants science authority to pronounce on what is real, true, objective and rational ("facts") while relegating ethics and religion to the realm of subjective opinion and nonrational experience ("values"). This distinction turns out to be very useful for philosophical naturalists. Instead of arguing that religion is false, which would arouse public protest, they merely relegate it to the realm of values—which keeps the question of true and false off the table altogether. As Johnson wrote in his earlier book *The Wedge of Truth*, religion is consigned "to the private sphere, where illusory beliefs are acceptable 'if they work for you.' " In this way, the philosophical naturalist can put on a show of being tolerant and respectful toward religious belief without granting it the status of actual knowledge.

As the Intelligent Design Movement challenges naturalism in

science, it will challenge naturalism in theology and other fields as well, making it possible to restore religion and morality to the status of genuine knowledge. To quote again from *The Wedge of Truth*, we must "assert the existence of such a cognitive territory, and be prepared to defend it." We must bring theology back into the sphere of public, objective knowledge.

Modeling a New Approach to Cultural Engagement

If Christians need to get out of the naturalist's chair in their professional convictions, they also need to get out of it in their day-to-day practices and strategies. Here again Johnson has led the way by modeling a new style of leadership.

For example, Johnson actively maintains friendships with leading atheistic evolutionists. Other Christian leaders may talk about having an impact on the wider culture, but in many cases their own lives have become circumscribed by the evangelical subculture. They amass large staffs and jet around the country speaking at conferences, spending much of their time with supporters and donors. By contrast, Johnson has no staff and remains on the cutting edge of contact with the secular world, keeping up personal friendships with many leading evolutionary thinkers. One video ("Darwinism: Science or Naturalistic Philosophy") features a Stanford University debate between Johnson and a die-hard evolutionist, William Provine of Cornell, who astonishes the audience by commenting that the two of them are really great friends and that after the debate they'll go out and have a drink together. Even as Johnson achieves a high profile within evangelicalism, he continues to do real, front-line work in confronting the secular culture.

At the same time, Johnson is building up a movement equipped to carry on the cause into the next generation. In the book *Boiling Point*, researchers George Barna and Mark Hatch note that many parachurch organizations today are built around personalities. As the celebrities pass from the scene, their organizations decline and die with them. But Johnson has refused to adopt the celebrity model. As he said at a recent conference, "One of the things that the Christian world is notorious for is a celebrity style of dealing with issues. That puts a big burden on one person. I never wanted a movement like that."

Instead, Johnson has developed a strategy summed up in his trademark metaphor of the wedge. Because of his position at the University of California at Berkeley and his considerable intellectual gifts, Johnson has functioned as the "thin edge" of a wedge, making an initial crack in the "log" of scientific naturalism. But he has known from the start that the thin edge cannot do the work alone. For his wedge to be successful the opening breakthrough has to be followed by the "thick edge" of the wedge—an expanding group of scientists, scholars and writers fanning out behind the leader. A single high-profile celebrity might succeed in attracting money and media attention, but it takes a large-scale movement to bring about an intellectual revolution.

How does one go about building such a movement? Religion reporter Terry Mattingly published a profile of Johnson that nicely summarizes his modus operandi. To begin with, "Johnson writes his own books" (unlike many big-name Christians who put their names on works written by others). In addition, he lends his name and reputation to help colleagues in the movement develop a higher profile and an independent voice of their own. As Mattingly writes, Johnson is constantly "promoting [books] written by his colleagues" and "he keeps yielding the stage" to them at public events. Johnson even procures funding for colleagues' book and research projects, and he helped establish the Discovery Institute as an institutional base for the movement. He recognizes the importance of raising up as many voices as possible, each credible in his or her own right, speaking to various aspects of intelligent design.

This is genuinely revolutionary, and it deserves to be held up as a more authentic model of Christian leadership, a practical application of the doctrine of the body of Christ: Those who are natural leaders have not been given leadership gifts by God to build a personal legacy but to build up the rest of the body. Our gifts are meant to serve not our own image and reputation but our fellow believers.

Johnson has charted this new course because he is sitting in the supernaturalist's chair; his sights have been lifted above personal ambition and reputation. As he puts it, he is motivated by "truth and justice." Yet, he adds with a sly grin, he also "wants to win." And winning takes a broad-based movement. By rejecting the celebrity model—by building up others instead of seeking to absorb their gifts and calling into his own persona—Johnson is nurturing a movement that will carry the cause forward into the next generation. As Mattingly writes, he "is convinced that aiming the spotlight at others is good strategy. He wants his cause to thrive after he is gone."

Demonstrating Spiritual Authenticity

Johnson's decision to sit in the supernaturalist's chair in both the content and method of his ministry is not a result of superior intellectual insight. It stems from spiritual humility and brokenness. Here we touch on the heart of who Phil Johnson is as a person. It is easy for Christians in the public spotlight to conceal their inner lives in order to maintain an invincible external image. Who can afford to be spiritually broken, or to face serious faults or failings, when one has a PR machine to keep cranking? Funds to raise? Donors to impress?

But Johnson has charted a different course—or more accurately God gave him an opportunity for spiritual growth that he could not refuse. In the pages that follow, Johnson describes a spiritual crisis he recently underwent, when a stroke brought him face to face with the possibility of losing some of his mental functions. This was potentially devastating for a man who lives by his intellect, who has won academic honors for his intelligence and whose greatest achievements have been in the life of the mind. He writes: "I wondered if I would ever lecture again, or write for publication."

This is the way spiritual crises typically come—in the form of loss and disappointment, and the fear and grief that accompany them. We rarely put our deepest trust in the Lord until we face the loss of what we rely on most. Scripture calls it dying to the world. We may believe all the right things. We may conscientiously do all the right things. We may garner all the trappings of success or even be in Christian ministry. But we will not experience true inner transformation until whatever we really live for is shattered, and we are willing to die—willing to give up everything we have loved and lived for, and to cast ourselves completely on the Lord.

For Johnson, that meant primarily his intellectual achievements. "I had always prided myself on being self-reliant, and my brain was what I had relied on," he writes. "Of all the bad things that might have happened to me, brain damage was the one I had feared most." In these pages, we can trace Johnson's dawning realization that the Lord's hand is at work even in suffering and loss. He begins to understand how suffering may be, as it was for Job, an episode in the invisible conflict in the heavenly realms between God and Satan. When we are "sifted like wheat," we can come out with a stronger, more resilient faith. Facing loss, we are struck by how temporal, broken, incomplete and contingent everything in this world is—and we experience an awakening hunger for the transcendent and eternal. God often has to cause our own plans to founder before we can see that he has much bigger plans than anything we hoped or dreamed.

This is the stuff of spiritual growth, but it takes a courageous man to admit it publicly. Instead of buffing and polishing his public persona, Phil writes frankly about his worries and weakness. He describes with admirable honesty the fears, uncertainties and sense of helplessness brought on by his stroke. He talks candidly about outbursts of anger and frustration. Most important, he reveals his growing understanding of his own spiritual need. He came to realize that since his conversion he has been what might be called "a recovering rationalist"—someone who is "not so much a believer in Christ as a skeptic about everything else."

What an apt phrase, and no doubt it applies to many of us. Certainly for a time after my own conversion, all I cared to read were books on apologetics and cultural criticism. Like Johnson, I was a "recovering rationalist" who stood *against* competing intellectual systems more than I stood *for* Christianity in all its fullness. It is usually only through personal crises that we are led more deeply into a living trust of the personal God we are so eager to proclaim.

Focusing on the Right Questions

By getting people to focus on the right questions—about science, theology, strategy, faith—Johnson has turned a sterile battleground into a fruitful conversation. This book may well serve as guide for Christians in other fields and disciplines across the board as they too learn how to ask the right questions.

Nancy Randolph Pearcey
June 2002

Introduction

THE LOGICAL TRAIN

In a lifetime of studying and participating in controversies, I have learned that the best way to approach a problem of any kind is usually not to talk or even think very much about the ultimate answer until I have made sure that I am asking all the right questions in the right order. When I am too eager to get to the answer, I may overlook some of the preliminary questions because I do not stop to reflect on why they are important and assume carelessly that I must already have answered them.

Similarly, when I want to persuade a lecture audience, I must be very careful to ensure that the audience understands the question correctly before I try to supply an answer. I am often misunderstood because some people who hear that I am lecturing on evolution assume from the title that I must be urging my audience to believe the Bible rather than science. They have been taught all their lives that no one but ignorant Bible-thumpers ever questions Darwin's theory, and they find it much easier to continue with that assumption than to make the effort to learn that there is another way to approach the subject. In consequence, they pay no attention to my careful explanation that I will be discussing only the definition of science and the strength or weakness of the scientific evidence that is cited in the literature to support the Darwinian claims. At the first opportunity, the people who have not paid attention to my description of the issue will start proclaiming that the Bible is not a science textbook, that the earth is billions of years old and that the whole controversy was settled in 1925 by the Scopes trial, which they know about only from the thoroughly fictional treatment of it in the play *Inherit the Wind.*

My problem is not persuading readers or hearers that I have the correct answers to the questions I am asking. My problem is rather to persuade those listeners and readers that the questions I am asking are the ones *they* should be asking, and that their education to this point has prepared them to ask the wrong questions rather than the right ones. If I begin an essay by trying to state the answers before making sure that my readers understand the questions, I have only myself to blame when they misunderstand. Likewise, if a reader assumes that he understands the question before he has read my explanation of why I start with some questions rather than others, that reader is not giving himself a fair chance to learn from what he is reading. Trying to get to the answer before one has understood all the right questions is a prime source of error in human affairs.

If I start with the right beginning question and let the answer to that first question suggest the next question and so on through each succeeding step, then the irresistible power of logic will eventually take me to the correct conclusion, even if at first that conclusion seems to be a very long way off. I use a railroad metaphor to explain how it works. If the train is up to full speed, and it is on the logical tracks, nothing can stop it from getting to the end of the line except a derailment. The logical train may also be irresistible when the tracks point in the wrong direction and the destination at the end of the line is something no one wanted to reach or ever anticipated reaching when the tracks were laid down and the train started to move slowly ahead on them.

For example, when law reformers in the 1960s liberalized the law of divorce, in the process they transformed marriage (at least as it's understood legally) from a sacred bond to a mere civil contract voidable at the option of either party. Although the reformers did not intend to approve same-sex marriage and probably never conceived of it as a possibility, a sufficiently far-sighted person could have seen that the tracks were headed in that direction. Probably the reformers would have rebuked such a person for opposing liberalized divorce on specious grounds. Now that the train has picked up a great deal of momentum, anyone can see that it is headed toward approval of gay marriage. The train will eventually get to that destination whether most people like it or not, unless some very strenuous work is done to move the tracks and point them in a different direction. Trying to stop the train by standing in its path is a good way to get run over.

Another thing to keep in mind is that what appears to be a setback, or even a disaster, may actually be a blessing in disguise if it forces us to reassess the direction in which we are headed and make sure that the tracks are pointed toward a destination we want to reach. That is why each crisis is also an opportunity to learn, and why we may not know before we reach the end of the line whether any particular experience was ultimately for good or for evil. Whenever the jolts of life force us to ask the right questions instead of the wrong ones, the experience is likely to be beneficial, even when it's painful. In this book I will explain how I learned the truth of that belief.

The first chapters establish a pattern of beginning with a text and then discussing three "right questions" about that text. However, I do not always keep to that pattern in the following chapters. The experiences that taught me to ask the right questions often came as a surprise, and some of that surprise effect is retained in the format of the chapters.

ONE

Biology and Liberal Freedom

THE HUMAN GENOME PROJECT
AND THE MEANING OF LIFE

The Santorum Amendment

On June 13, 2001, U.S. Senator Rick Santorum (Rep., PA) proposed a two-sentence amendment to the White House-sponsored education bill that was under consideration in Congress. The Santorum Amendment said simply that "it is the sense of the Senate that (1) good science education should prepare students to distinguish the data or testable theories of science from philosophical or religious claims that are made in the name of science; and (2) where biological evolution is taught, the curriculum should help students to understand why this subject generates so much continuing controversy and should prepare the students to be informed participants in public discussions regarding the subject."

Senator Santorum explained that as a mere "sense of the Senate" resolution, the amendment included no provisions for implementation or enforcement and hence would not require or fund educators to do anything in particular. It merely acknowledged the

existence of disagreements and controversies over scientific theories, especially biological evolution, and supported the conclusion
that science education would be more effective if it prepared students to understand these controversies. Senator Santorum then
yielded the floor to Senator Edward Kennedy, who was taking the
leading role on the bill for the Democrats. Senator Kennedy enthusiastically agreed with Senator Santorum, urging all senators to
vote for the amendment because "we want children to be able to
talk about different concepts and do it intelligently with the best
information that is before them." After additional supporting
statements from other senators, the amendment passed by a huge
bipartisan majority of 91-8.

One might have expected mainstream organizations of scientists and science educators to take the same view that Senator
Kennedy had expressed and to welcome the amendment as an
invitation to educate the public to understand science as the scientists do. Although I drafted the amendment for Senator Santorum, it did not give any recognition to dissenters from
Darwinian orthodoxy such as myself, so the existing science educators would have had a free hand to present the subject as they
thought best. Instead these organizations vehemently opposed the
amendment and exerted all their influence in an attempt to persuade the legislators to drop it from the final version of the bill.

They almost succeeded: the House of Representatives passed
the education bill without a parallel "sense of the House" resolution, but the amendment attracted support from both House and
Senate members of the Conference Committee, which had the task
of reconciling the House and Senate bills. The science educators'

principal, explicit objection to the Santorum Amendment was that it singled out biological evolution as a subject of controversy. They insisted that there was no *scientific* controversy over evolution but merely a religiously or politically based resistance to scientific knowledge, which should not be dignified by allowing it to be expressed in science classes.

Their logic seems to have been that the many persons with impressive scientific credentials who have expressed skepticism toward the theory of evolution must not really be scientists, since they have expressed skepticism toward the theory of evolution. More important, the Darwinist educators cannot afford to acknowledge to either their students or the public that there *is* a distinction between the data or testable theories of science, on the one hand, and philosophical or religious claims that are made in the name of science, on the other. All Darwinist propaganda depends on blurring that distinction so that a credulous public is taught to accept philosophical naturalism/materialism as inherent in the definition of "science." On that premise scientific knowledge is deemed the least implausible naturalistic mechanism for creating complex life and therefore true. Sometimes Darwinists say that their naturalism is merely methodological and makes no claims about reality, but of course the method is thought to be sound because it is deemed to reflect reality.

Public opinion polls consistently show that a very substantial proportion of the American public is skeptical of the theory of evolution—at least when it is offered as a complete explanation for the history of life—a skepticism that scientific organizations deplore. How is public skepticism over evolution ever to be addressed unless educators recognize its existence and use their best efforts to educate the public in the errors in the public's way of thinking? Education in other subjects aims at helping students to understand the subject as completely as possible. However, education in biological evolution (Darwinism) must aim at keeping the students and the general public confused so they will continue to accept philosophy as science and not perceive that the scientific evidence is not consistent with the *scientistic* philosophy (naturalism) that the ruling metaphysicians of science want them to believe. Darwinism and clear thinking are at odds with each other.

In the end the amendment survived virtually unchanged in the report of the Conference Committee, which was approved by both houses of Congress with the final version of the education bill, signed by President Bush in January 2002. The Conference Committee report is not itself an operative provision of the statute, but it is the primary source of legislative history to which a judge or administrator would turn to interpret the meaning of key terms that *are* operative in the statute, like *science* and *education*. What I had hoped to accomplish with the language of the amendment was primarily to make it very difficult for public school authorities to justify firing or disciplining a teacher who informs students of the weaknesses of the Darwinian theory, rather than teaching it in the authoritarian and dogmatic manner that Darwinians have been able to enforce up until now. Beyond that, how much effect the amendment may have depends on what the public makes of it. If people at the grassroots level are active in raising objections to Darwinian dogmatism, the amendment will protect their legal position. If the people allow themselves to be cowed by the authority of the current rulers of "science," then Darwinian dogmatism will go on much as it did before the amendment was passed.

To understand why educators find biological evolution so difficult an issue to handle, it will be helpful to consider the differing interpretations in the media of the first results of the massive Human Genome Project, probably the most ambitious biological research effort in history. Unless people keep their common sense firmly under wraps, most instinctively recognize that a supernatural intelligence must be at work in the wonders of biology. It takes years of indoctrination to learn to ignore the evidence of intelligent design that is so apparent before our very eyes.

The Human Genome Project and What It Means to Be Human

On June 26, 2000, President Clinton announced that the scientific effort to sequence the human genome had met with its first substantial success. Scientists warned that it might be a long time before tangible benefits like cures for diseases resulted, but the accomplishment nonetheless generated a mixture of elation and suspicion. Elimination of genetic diseases like cystic fibrosis obviously would be desirable if it could be achieved, but the program of the more ambitious genetic wizards goes well beyond curing or preventing specific diseases. They yearn to produce better people by redesigning the human genome, which they take to be a cobbled-together product of unguided natural evolutionary processes consisting largely of "junk DNA" along with a smaller number of genes that code for proteins.

Whatever technologies the scientists invent will inevitably be for sale in the amoral international marketplace, where enforcement of any ethical restraints may be extremely difficult. For example, parents who can afford to pay may one day be able to purchase genetic makeovers that could enable them to have "designer children" who are healthier and smarter than those of their less affluent neighbors, thus perpetuating a genetic caste system. The promised biotech wonders may be a long time in coming, but in the very near future, information from genetic testing may be used to make some persons unemployable or ineligible for insurance coverage.

President Clinton tried to provide some reassurance against these widely recognized dangers, vowing that "as we consider how to use new discoveries, we must also not retreat from our oldest and most cherished human values." Specifically, the President said, "All of us are created equal, entitled to equal treatment under the law." Created? The claim that all humans are created equal is a creationist notion that implies other species are inferior, presumably because only humans bear the image of the Creator. president Clinton did not mention the possibility, now widely advocated or even taken for granted in elite scientific and philosophical circles, that what biologists are telling us about life and evolution has made our oldest and most cherished values obsolete. For example, many scientists and philosophers now say that to award a special status to human beings (that is, to "us") is an anthropocentric sin called *speciesism*, akin to racism and sexism. The core message of evolutionary biology is that humans are not created at all, much less created in the image of God, but are merely a random product of evolution like every other species. In that case, to declare humans to have some unique status above that of other species may be as arbitrary as to declare one race of human beings superior to the others.

This challenge to human pretensions to superiority comes from biological evolutionary theory, but its philosophical implications are causing immense difficulty for biologists by inspiring the growth of an animal rights movement that does not accept the legitimacy of animal experimentation. The issue of animal testing first arose with respect to those animals that are most similar to man, such as chimpanzees, but the logic has been extended even to laboratory rats and beyond. In consequence laboratories that use animals for experiments have had to become fortresses, and the scientists fear for their very lives. None of this is surprising if you take seriously the premise that experimentation on animals is morally equivalent to performing the same experiments on human beings.

Insofar as the genome project leads to further findings of similarities between men and animals, it may have the ironic effect of encouraging further acts of terrorism against biologists. However that story may develop, the formal celebration of the initial success of the genetic sequencing provided evidence that creationist premises remain influential even in the vehemently materialist culture of biology. President Clinton exulted that "today, we are learning the language in which God created life; we are gaining ever more awe for the complexity, the beauty, the wonder of God's most divine and sacred gift." Dr. Francis S. Collins, the scientific director of the government's Human Genome Project, used similar words, saying, "It is humbling for me and awe-inspiring to realize that we have caught the first glimpse of our own instruction book, previously known only to God."

Taken at face value, these statements seem to say that genome research actually *supports* the view that a supernatural mind designed the instructions that guide the immensely complex biochemical processes of life. To put the same point negatively, Clinton and Collins seemed to be repudiating the central claim of evolutionary naturalism, which is that exclusively natural causes like chance and physical law produced all the features of life, including whatever "instructions" are contained in DNA. Whatever Clinton and Collins may think about the matter, however, the vast majority of biologists, especially prestigious biologists, emphatically deny that God had anything to do with evolution, and contemptuously dismiss what they call "intelligent design creationism" as inherently unacceptable to science, regardless of the evidence.

For example, Dr. David Baltimore, a Nobel laureate and president of the California Institute of Technology, wrote in the *New York Times* that the genome project had revealed that "our genes look very much like those of fruit flies, worms and even plants." Baltimore argued that this finding implies that "we are all descended from the same humble beginnings," which he thought "should be, but won't be, the end of creationism" (David Baltimore, "50,000 Genes, and We Know Them All [Almost]," *New York Times,* June 25, 2000).

Because current scientific doctrine holds that the genes contain a sort of recipe for creating a human, Dr. Baltimore's logic seems to imply that discovery of those genetic similarities should put an end both to the idea that humans (or other organisms) were created and to the idea that *Homo sapiens* is sufficiently different from other organisms to merit any unique status. So much for the traditional, theology-based view that humans are all created equal to each other and superior to everything else.

Another genome scientist wrote to the *New York Times* that President Clinton's references to a language in which God created life "could not be further from the truth," and that these words would only "give more ammunition to creationists to further their destructive social and political agenda" ("Eureka! A Key to the Code of Life," *New York Times*, June 28, 2000). The scientist did not say what that destructive agenda is, but by raising this objection he implied the possibility that biologists may reject the concept of design in biology because they dislike the possible religious, political or moral implications rather than because their data compel that conclusion. In that case, the rest of us may wonder where biologists got the idea that they should have authority over religion, politics and morality, and whether they may turn out to be the ones who are furthering a destructive social and political agenda.

Some scientists seemed much more receptive to the idea that the evidence from the genome project points to an intelligent designer. Gene Myers, a computer scientist who was instrumental in assembling the genome map for Celera Corporation, told a science reporter for the *San Francisco Chronicle,* "What really astounds me is the architecture of life. The system is extremely complex. It's like it was designed. . . . There's a huge intelligence there. I don't see that as being unscientific. Others may, but not me" (Tom Abate, "Human Genome Map Has Scientists Talking About the Divine: Surprisingly Low Number of Genes Raises Big Questions," *San Francisco Chronicle*, February 19, 2001).

Abate was also astonished to discover that the geneticists were estimating that the total content of the human genome amounts to only about thirty thousand genes, approximately the same as the mouse genome. Larger estimates have since appeared, but the underlying problem remains: it is an interesting fact that our genes look very much like those of fruit flies, worms and even plants, but this fact does nothing to explain why humans are so different from fruit flies, worms and plants. If identifiable genetic differences do not account for our uniquely human characteristics, then perhaps the true lesson of the Human Genome Project is that genes are not nearly as important as we have been led to believe. This possibility must be very disquieting to investors who anticipate huge profits from the exploitation of technologies for manipulating all the uniquely human genes that haven't been found.

Knowledge and Belief

One might expect that there would be a healthy debate in intellectual circles over whether the appearance of design in biology is real or illusory, and how the evidence of biology may bear on the proposition that humans are created equal to each other and superior to all other forms of life. The reason that debate does not occur is that the intellectual culture of our time enforces a distinction between belief and knowledge, and between faith and reason, which makes it virtually impossible to ask the right questions.

The difference between belief and knowledge is easy to state but often subtle in application. Knowledge is objective and valid for everyone; belief is subjective and valid only for the believer. One rough way of expressing the distinction is that knowledge may be taught in the public schools and universities or used as a foundation for law making, whereas beliefs are confined to private life— unless they are beliefs that have the approval of the cognitive elite, which claims the power to draw the boundary between belief and knowledge.

The paradigmatic illustration of the distinction is the assumed contrast between scientific *knowledge* and religious *belief,* supplemented by the parallel contrast between scientific *reason* and religious *faith,* which rationalists assume to mean belief without reasons. The fundamental rule of cognitive modernism is that every rational person accepts scientific knowledge because it is by definition based on reason and evidence, even if the evidence can't be produced and the reasons seem unreasonable to many, whereas religious belief is at most optional because it is conclusively presumed to be based merely on subjective preference or indoctrination. Persons who internalize these distinctions automatically classify references to God as nonrational and hence not to be taken seriously as truth claims, although they may have to be treated tactfully for political reasons.

Following the same logic, guidelines for teaching science in the public schools routinely specify that science is committed to explaining all phenomena in terms of natural causes only. In strict logic this leaves open the possibility that some phenomena (such as the DNA instruction book) really are the products of supernatural causes and hence cannot be fully explained by a science pre-committed to naturalism. In practice modernist intellectuals are extremely reluctant to concede such a possibility because to the naturalistic mindset that conclusion implies "giving up on science" and embracing ignorance.

Because philosophical naturalism is thus incorporated in the very definition of *science,* most biologists think it is as much a scientific fact that the genome is the product of natural causes alone as it is that DNA is composed of organic chemicals. Hence science cannot recognize an instruction book in the genome other than in a metaphorical sense, because an unevolved intelligence capable of writing instructions would be supernatural. As one naive biology professor explained in a letter to *Nature,* the world's most prominent scientific journal, "Even if all the data point to an intelligent designer, such an hypothesis is excluded from science because it is not naturalistic" (Scott C. Todd, "A View from Kansas on That Evolution Debate," *Nature,* September 30, 1999, p. 423).

More politically sophisticated biologists do not express themselves so candidly because they know what the hated creationists would make of the admission that biologists sometimes disregard the data if it points in a direction they consider unacceptable on philosophic grounds. More commonly, scientific naturalists simply invoke the cultural power of "science" to confirm the claim that the evidence supports their philosophical position, even when the evidence consists of nothing more than similarities between various kinds of organisms. One could employ the same logic to prove that the nine symphonies of Beethoven had no composer since they all employ similar musical elements.

Individual scientists who do believe in a supernatural reality had better be careful to keep their religion safely insulated from their scientific responsibilities. The professional ethos on this subject was nicely encapsulated in a *Scientific American* magazine profile of Dr. Francis Collins, the director of the Human Genome Project who shared the stage with President Clinton. Collins is an evangelical Christian who publicly identifies himself as such, and this is a curiosity indeed for a scientist at such a prestigious level. In what the editors probably intended as a display of tolerance, they lauded Collins because he "strives to keep his Christianity from interfering with his science and politics." Of course, the same editors would never write a similar sentence about an atheist, such as that "Richard Lewontin strives to keep his atheism, his Jewishness and his Marxism from interfering with his science and politics." Lewontin, a Harvard genetics professor who occupies a place near the top of the scientific pyramid, wears his atheism, his ethnicity and his politics on his sleeve. A member of a disfavored group had better not think he can get away with the same thing.

It may seem that Collins *did* let his Christianity interfere with his science when he referred to that "instruction book previously known only to God," but the circumstances were exceptional. On ceremonial occasions directors of expensive scientific programs are allowed wide latitude to say whatever is necessary to please the taxpayers who have to pay the bill. If Collins were to deliver a lecture on God's instruction book at a scientific meeting, arguing that the information content of the genome points to an author, the reaction would be ferocious.

The Right Questions About Science, God and Morality

❶ Is it wrong to mix science and religion, or is such mixing inescapable?

In 1981 the U.S. National Academy of Sciences resolved that "religion and science are separate and mutually exclusive realms of human thought whose presentation in the same context leads to misunderstanding of both scientific theory and religious belief." As with the supposed "scientific finding" that humans have no unique moral or spiritual status, the scientists intended the resolution to be nothing more than a weapon for use against creationists. They apparently gave no thought to the larger implications—whether it is even possible to avoid religious implications altogether when explaining the origins of human life. In fact prestigious scientists continually publish books that so thoroughly mix the two subjects that the word *god* or *gods* even appears in the title, a practice that is well known to boost sales and consequent royalties. For example, see *The Genetic Gods: Evolution and Belief in Human Affairs* by Dr. John C. Advise (Cambridge, Mass.: Harvard University Press, 2001). Dr. Advise, a scientific materialist who thinks his philosophy is required by "science," writes in the preface, "I hope to diminish the hostility between these differing epistemological approaches (theology and evolutionary biology), [and I also] hope to resolve a central issue in my own life: how to reconcile the intellectual demands and pleasures of critical scientific thought with the sense of purpose and fulfillment that a rich spiritual life can provide."

When a materialist proposes a reconciliation of science with religion, the terms of the peace proposal usually amount to a demand for unconditional surrender. The theologians must accept the genetic gods in place of the old God, whose mention is banned not only from science but also from ethical discourse, including the ethics of employing genetic technology. According to Advise:

> The many ethical challenges prompted by the new genetic technol-
> ogies are both complex and profound. In response, not only scien-
> tists, theologians, and lawmakers, but everyone must gather at the
> discussion table to consider rational, humanitarian courses of
> action. In such deliberations, perhaps the only mode of argument
> to be firmly censored—the only 'wrong' approach—is that in
> which the moral authority of a god is asserted. As judged by the
> diversity of opinions held by responsible individuals on ethical
> matters pertaining to the human condition, any supernatural deity
> either has been strangely silent on such issues or else has conveyed
> vastly different messages to different listeners.

**❷ If God is dead, is everything permitted, or does moral judgment
continue as before but on a secular basis?**

The early modernist rationalists assumed that the death of God was merely the death of superstition. On that premise modernist man, guided by science, could preserve the best of the old moral-ity (or President Clinton's "oldest and most cherished human val-ues") in a revised moral code founded on the solid rock of enlightened secular reason. More recently many have come to doubt that human reason can supply the missing transcendent standard by which differing human moral beliefs can be evaluated. From a scientific standpoint, morality—like religion—is a matter of subjective belief rather than objective knowledge. That makes it effectively a matter of personal preference. This does not mean that moral codes will cease to exist (even a gang of robbers or terrorists has one), but it does mean that those codes will be grounded on the preferences of local power holders rather than on universal principles of reason and knowledge. What is right or wrong depends on the preference of whoever has the power to impose his will.

Perhaps no one should have that power, and every individual should have an absolute right to choice. That is the alternative that three centrist justices of the U.S. Supreme Court seemed to embrace in 1992 when they reaffirmed the existence of a constitutional right to abortion. In what lawyers call the "mystery passage," the justices wrote, "At the heart of liberty is the right to define one's own concept of existence, of meaning, of the universe, and of the mystery of human life. Beliefs about these matters could not define the attributes of personhood were they formed under compulsion of the State" (*Planned Parenthood of Southeastern Pennsylvania v. Casey,* 505 U.S. 833 [1992], 851 [opinion by Justices O'Connor, Kennedy and Souter]). However, no American law, including laws restricting abortion, seeks to compel "beliefs about these matters." The only question presented by abortion prohibitions is whether a person is entitled to *act* on his or her beliefs when the action involves a taking of innocent human life.

An affirmative answer to *that* question would seem to justify assassination and even mass murder. Of course, the justices did not mean to endorse such a broad proposition, so they immediately qualified the general language by saying that the right to act on such ultimate beliefs applies only to a woman who is deciding whether or not to bear a child or terminate the pregnancy. In such a case, "the destiny of the woman must be shaped to a large extent on her own conception of her spiritual imperatives and her place in society." Thus a court influenced or intimidated by feminist ideology granted—only to one kind of person in one kind of situation—a right to act on her beliefs even at the cost of human life. Readers will readily imagine, however, that many others will think this restriction arbitrary and will wish to extend the same logic to claim a broader privilege for themselves.

❸ Is God safely buried, or should we anticipate a resurrection?

The question is not whether some form of "religious belief" will continue, because it surely will, but whether God will always be excluded from the cognitive realm of knowledge and thus remain confined in the never-never land of subjective belief where Zeus, Thor and Santa Claus are to be found. If God is nothing more than a concept in the human mind and has no power to act or speak for himself, then it may seem that man created God and has the power to dispense with his own creation. The right question then is not so much whether God exists as whether the Word of God exists and whether that Word has done something that truth-seekers cannot afford to ignore. These issues are discussed in my previous book *The Wedge of Truth* (Downers Grove, Ill.: InterVarsity Press, 2000), especially chapter seven. I expect there will be a great deal more discussion along these lines as truth-seekers take advantage of the liberal principles of the Santorum Amendment once they fully grasp the religious and philosophical dimensions of the nihilistic philosophy that has seized control of our culture in the name of science.

TWO

The Word of God in Education

Visits to Two Universities

Until recently educators assumed that controversy over biological evolution was a thing of the past, but now the subject is coming to life on both Christian and secular campuses. I saw this firsthand in November 2000 when I lectured at a Christian college and at a Midwestern state university. I came to South Dakota State University to give that university's endowed Harding Lecture, a rare opportunity for me to accept the kind of honor and honorarium that is usually extended only to a celebrity, generally one whose message or reason for notoriety fits the prejudices of the arbiters of academic fashion. Previous Harding lecturers have included Ralph Nader, former British prime minister Sir Harold Wilson, John Dean, Betty Friedan, Molly Ivins and Senator Tom Daschle. I indulge in this name dropping not because I am flattered to be classed with antiheroes like Watergate conspirator John Dean or the feminist icon Betty Friedan but to note the encouraging fact

that it has become possible for a notorious "intelligent design creationist" to be selected by a faculty committee at a secular university for a prestigious lectureship, albeit the university in question
is far from the top of the academic pecking order.

Committee members told me that one reason I was selected was
that attendance at these lectures tends to be embarrassingly low,
and they knew that my message would generate enough interest
to fill an auditorium. This is an important point. It is of course
desirable that a message be true, but the truth will not be heard
unless the lecturer is sufficiently interesting not only to draw an
audience but to disarm some of their prejudices so they will pay
attention to what they are hearing and then think about it a little
afterward. When I speak, my goal is not to convince audiences
that my position is correct but to have people leave the auditorium
saying something like, "There is more to this controversy than I
thought. We ought to be discussing these issues in the classroom."

In the hope of opening up the ideologically closed classroom
environment a little, I ask groups or individuals that want me to
speak at a particular university to try to arrange a "front door" invitation, with sponsorship from an academic department and an
introduction by some highly respected professor or administrator.
I know that the label "visiting Christian lecturer" by itself signifies
to secular professors that "this is the kind of speaker we tolerate
on campus to demonstrate our broad-mindedness, but not somebody whom we would ever take seriously." Once I do get on the
platform however, I usually find it fairly easy to evoke the right
kind of interest, even if the academic authorities refuse to cooper-
ate.

In every university there are scores of faculty and students who are suffocated by the prevailing dogmas of scientific materialism or political correctness but who almost never get a chance to hear anything else. Conditions are ripe for a reformation, but somebody has to take the lead in introducing new ideas into a professorial culture that desperately wants to keep them out. That very desperation creates a sense of excitement when somebody finally does break through the barriers and promotes the excluded concepts in language that makes sense within the academic environment. In fact, I use practically the same arguments against Darwinism and scientific materialism that the nineteenth-century Darwinists used against the established prejudices of their day. "You ought to pay attention to our scientific evidence," they said, "even if it contradicts your Scriptures and your philosophical presuppositions." Darwinists cannot afford to agree to that proposal, because their essential presupposition is, as it always has been, that it is self-contradictory to speak of scientific evidence against materialism, since a commitment to materialism as a methodology is inherent in the very definition of "science." On the other hand, Darwinists are embarrassed to argue that a philosophical doctrine takes precedence over empirical evidence because this assertion also contradicts the essence of science.

The red carpet treatment I received at South Dakota State contrasted with the courteous but wary reception I encountered at about the same time at a Christian (Nazarene) college. The secular university had invited me to give an endowed lecture because the lecture committee welcomed the excitement of a challenge to accepted ways of thinking. The Christian college, however, welcomed me only reluctantly, at the insistence of a dedicated young science teacher who had offered to cover the costs out of his own pocket. Christian colleges generally do not welcome an outside speaker who addresses the conflict between creation and evolution. There are exceptions. For example, at one Christian college in Indiana, biology professors took the lead in arranging an invitation for me to spend two days with the entire faculty at their beginning-of-the-year retreat. An invitation involving sustained faculty discussion about creation and naturalism is highly unusual, however. Most Christian college professors are as hostile to the "religious right" as their secular counterparts. They want to have as little as possible to do with controversies over evolution, seeing the whole subject as inherently connected to a know-nothing fundamentalism that has hindered Christian institutions from improving their academic quality and standing.

The problem of academic standing stems primarily from the fact that the agnostic professors who dominate the academic culture tend to have a low opinion of anything labeled "Christian." This puts professors at Christian colleges under pressure to distance themselves from anything that sounds even remotely like "fundamentalism"—that being just about the most negative word in the academic vocabulary. Nothing sounds so much like fundamentalism as a challenge to the theory of evolution.

Christian college professors have to serve two very demanding and inconsistent masters. On the one hand, trustees and tuition-paying parents tend to think that the professors ought to teach in a way that reinforces orthodox Christian doctrines and thus keep the students secure in the faith they learned in their homes and churches. On the other hand, the same parents and trustees want the colleges to have reasonably good academic ratings so that the degrees they confer will have some value for such things as graduate school applications.

These two objectives stand in considerable tension because academic standing is conferred by the secular accrediting agencies and the academic associations for the various disciplines. The best-credentialed Christian professors will have earned graduate degrees at universities where naturalism and rationality are assumed to be inseparable, and thereafter they will go up or down the academic pecking order, depending on their standing with mostly secular peers. There is every incentive for them to assume that Christian faith is no more than a veneer spread thinly over the kind of learning that they experienced in graduate school and that they practice in secular academic gatherings. If the parents and trustees understood precisely what these professors were thinking and teaching, they might suspect that students were being taught to grow away from their childhood faith rather than to grow within it. Perhaps it would more realistic to say that their existing suspicions would be resoundingly confirmed.

The tension between Christian faith and academic rationalism is present in every subject, but the biology curriculum is ground zero. Christian professors have to teach evolution without reservation if they are to maintain any credibility with the secular biologists, but they have to affirm that they believe in divine creation to convince their religious community that they are more than nominally Christian. To receive their salaries, they often have to sign "faith statements" that say with greater or lesser specificity that they believe in creation as taught in the Bible. Even if the statement is vaguely worded, most of their Christian constituency assumes that *creation* implies at a minimum some supernatural influence in nature, a concept vehemently opposed in mainstream scientific circles.

The path of least resistance is to pretend that there is no conflict between evolutionary naturalism and Christian theism by redefining *evolution* to mean mere gradual change of some kind, ignoring the requirement that the change be undirected and purposeless. As one Christian college professor expressed it in a manuscript intended to soothe the faithful, biological evolutionists are merely saying that "God created gradually." That is utterly misleading, of course, because the biologists are really teaching that God had nothing to do with evolution. To be accepted in secular circles, a biologist must affirm—or at least not dispute—that evolution is a purposeless process that produced human beings by accident rather than by design. It is easy to see why most Christian professors don't want the implicit conflict to be brought to the surface.

Opening the Evangelical Mind

The pressures on Christian colleges from the secular academic side were illustrated in an article by sociologist Alan Wolfe in the October 2000 issue of the *Atlantic Monthly*, titled "The Opening of the Evangelical Mind." Wolfe began by bluntly observing that in the twentieth century, Protestant evangelicals ranked "dead last in intellectual stature." Recently, however, there are signs of renewed brain activity at evangelical colleges.

Signs that are encouraging to Wolfe, however, would be seen by many evangelicals as flags warning that the institutions are teetering on the edge of outright apostasy. Wolfe's first example was a political science class at Wheaton College (generally considered the academic flagship of the evangelical college world). The class discussed a Supreme Court decision which held that it is unconstitutional for a rabbi to give a nonsectarian prayer—offering thanks to God "for the legacy of America where diversity is celebrated and the rights of minorities are protected"—at a public school graduation ceremony.

The Wheaton students all took the standard "wall of separation" line, Wolfe reports, "as one might expect from a generation taught to believe that tolerance is the highest moral value." (In liberal academia God is always associated with intolerance, even when he endorses diversity and the rights of minorities.) When one student tried to criticize the majority opinion, the others "laughingly disagreed." Wolfe judged this demonstration of political correctness to be a "vigorous, intelligent, and informed" discussion. In ideology if not in sophistication, it seemed identical to what one would hear at a secular law school or a meeting of the American Civil Liberties Union.

Wolfe's description of Southern California's Fuller Theological Seminary was of a similar nature. It seems from Wolfe's report that the most noteworthy characteristic of Fuller's School of Psychology is its admiration, even sanctification, of the New Age author M. Scott Peck. According to Wolfe, Peck's writing reflects sympathy for a wide variety of Eastern religions and "argues for a capacious understanding of religion that need not even include a belief in God." Peck's ideas, and just about all other ideas, were accepted uncritically in Professor Jim Guy's class. According to Wolfe:

The discussion rarely moved beyond an exchange of cliches. But the class environment was as warm and caring as Peck's reassuring text. Every student's comment, no matter how trivial, was taken as a serious reflection on the human condition. (My impression, based on what I admit is an unrepresentative sample of classes, is that the ethos of Fuller makes it inconceivable that any professor would ever say that a student's comment was simply wrong.) . . . The students I spoke to after class, all of whom planned to become either ministers or mental-health professionals, loved the class and loved Guy. Their jobs will require them to maintain an optimistic outlook on the world, and Peck's spiritualism will come in handy when they are plagued with doubts.

It would be interesting to know how much tolerance a Fuller student would encounter if he or she argued that Fuller ought to be teaching traditional Christian doctrines rather than a post-Christian New Age spiritualism.

Perhaps Wolfe's anecdotes were not representative of the teaching at Wheaton or Fuller, but representatives of the institutions didn't offer any specific counterexamples when they responded to Wolfe's article online. Whatever is actually going on at these institutions, Wolfe's meant-to-be-favorable article sent a very clear message about what Christian colleges have to do to get any recognition from secular intellectuals. The message was that Christian professors may aspire to a kindly pat on the head from the kind of people who write for the *Atlantic Monthly*, but only to the extent that they move in the direction of secular liberalism or postmodernist relativism. In secular intellectual circles, distinctively Christian means distinctively inferior, whereas a warm and fuzzy environment where students are never wrong—unless they display "intolerance"—is evidence that things are at least going in the right direction.

Christian colleges also face pressures from the conservative side. These often involve such subjects as the regulation of student behavior. But in intellectual matters, biological evolution is where conflict is most likely to erupt. Should Christian college professors be required to teach that creation occurred more or less as described in the first three chapters of Genesis? Many of the tuition-paying parents probably think so, and being faced with such a requirement is a nightmare for professors who want to teach the kind of science that the mainstream scientific community regards as valid. The faculty at the Nazarene college was traumatized shortly before my own visit by a prominent proponent of young-earth creation science who insisted that creation in six literal days is a matter of fundamental importance to the Christian faith. He gave his audience the distinct impression that they must be on the way to abandoning the Christian faith altogether if they disputed the reliability of the Genesis account.

I have met many young-earth creationists and respect their position, whatever the world may think of it. They are dismissively called "Genesis literalists," but this is a caricature. They know that Genesis contains figures of speech, such as the reference to God walking in the garden. Creationists read Genesis not with a wooden literalism but by an interpretive principle that was standard everywhere before the rise of postmodernist innovations such as deconstruction and reader response theory: a text should be read as the author meant it to be read. For Christians there is an ideal reader available: Jesus himself. Where Jesus quoted Genesis, the meaning he took from the words is normative for all Christians. To say that Jesus didn't know about modern science is bad enough, but to say that he didn't even understand Genesis is fatal to Christianity if true, and blasphemous if false. So I readily concede that Genesis is important and that the question of its historical value cannot be evaded indefinitely. "What should we think of Genesis?" That is one of the right questions, and I will explore it in chapter six, but it is not the right place to begin.

How to interpret Genesis is the subject of very spirited debate even in the most conservative circles of evangelicalism. To tell professors that they all have to accept one position on a priori grounds is to tell many of them that they must teach what they believe to be false and to tell all of them that they must abandon all hope of being respected in the academic world. That is hardly the way to encourage them to bring up the difficult issues in the classroom or to engage in intellectual debate with other professors. If we want Christian professors to confront the difficult questions rather than to evade them, we have to assure them that they won't get their heads cut off if they say something that offends one or the other of the institution's constituencies. Academic freedom is not a luxury in higher education but a necessity. The underlying question is whether truth emerges from a fair-minded consideration of the evidence or from the pronouncements of whomever holds the power.

Attempts at top-down thought control are ultimately futile. Prescribing answers in advance of a free discussion produces only the *appearance* of compliance by teachers who will send an implicit message to students that "we only teach this stuff because we have to, and if we were free to do so, we would teach you something better."[*] The way to deal with timidity and self-deception in Christian education is not to try to prevent bad ideas from being taught but rather to ensure that the bad ideas are effectively countered by better ideas in an atmosphere of open deliberation. Conflicting pressures have unfortunately created an understandable desire among the academics to keep the peace by tolerating everybody except those who insist on rocking the boat. I want to rock that boat vigorously, but in a way that makes Christian education more confident and less fearful, that tells the people huddling in that boat to "come on in, the water's fine."

Unite the Pair So Long Disjoined

Where to begin was the problem in my mind as I stood up to speak about creation and evolution to the morning assembly at the Nazarene college, which follows the Wesleyan tradition. I was encouraged to learn that the college chaplain, who was to introduce me, understood what I would be saying so profoundly that he changed his introductory remarks to fit what he had learned from our preliminary conversation. Best of all, I saw an eloquent

---

[*]The aspect of Christian education that incurs the strongest disapproval from secular academics is the requirement of "faith statements," as mentioned earlier. Secular colleges have their own required doctrinal commitments, but they are enforced by the faculty itself, through peer review of publications and promotions rather than by trustees. The existence of those Christian faith statements does not mean that Christian colleges value academic freedom less than their secular counterparts. What it signifies is that left to themselves, Christian professors would drift away from whatever Christian doctrines are inconsistent with the fundamental assumptions of the secular academic world.

summary of my intended thesis written on the wall at the front of
the auditorium. The motto of this college, written by Charles Wesley, is "Unite the pair so long disjoined, knowledge and vital piety."
Indeed that *is* the perfect starting place: how are knowledge and
vital piety to be joined, assuming that they *should* be joined?

Most of my academic audiences think they already know what
the creation-evolution debate is about, and their misunderstanding keeps knowledge and piety disjoined. They think that the
debate is about the book of Genesis and about the conflict
between science and religion, or between reason and faith. They
are wrong. Most people have accepted a biased definition of the
conflict, a definition which assures that scientific naturalists will
win all the important arguments.

When I lecture the first problem I face is not convincing the
audience that I have the right answers but convincing them that
they have been asking the wrong questions. The conflict is not primarily about Genesis, nor does it involve a clash between science
and religion, or between reason and faith. It would be much more
accurate to say that it involves a clash between two religions and
two definitions of science. Once we define the questions correctly,
the opposing answers emerge as naturally as an apple falling from
a tree or a key fitting into a lock. The problem is to get past the
barrier of false understanding, which teaches us that the gulf
between the naturalistic and theistic starting points can be bridged
by a superficial compromise. It helps if I can package my message
in language that the audience already understands, language that
allows them to hear the substance without the burden of translat-
ing unfamiliar words into familiar concepts. Charles Wesley's lan-

guage was perfect for this purpose. Knowledge and piety: how *can* that disjoined pair be united, and should we even aspire to unite them? Here is the substance of what I said:

> All understanding starts with an understanding of creation. Knowledge has been *dis*united from piety because the two are understood to rest on radically different creation stories. On the one hand, the Bible teaches that we were created by an intelligent, purposeful being who cares about how we live our lives and has communicated to us through his Word. This is defined in our culture as religion. On the other hand, the secular world, claiming scientific authority for its doctrine, teaches us that we were created by nature, through a purposeless mechanism which combined random genetic change with the principle of differential reproduction. These two doctrines of creation are fundamentally opposed to each other. Which is correct?

If that is the right question to ask, then the wrong way to answer it is to start with the book of Genesis. Starting people in that direction leads to at least three fundamental errors.

First, people assume that the controversy involves mainly the time scale of Genesis. That leads many well-meaning Christians to think that they can resolve the controversy if they interpret the "days" of Genesis to be geological ages of indefinite length. But the *first* question is not whether the historical details of Genesis are true but whether the fundamental meaning of Genesis is true. If we go to the historical details before we understand the fundamental meanings, we invite misunderstanding.

Second, those well-meaning Christians tend to assume that the theory of evolution threatens only the early chapters of the book of Genesis. If that is all that is at stake, what does it matter? Perhaps Christians can afford to align Genesis with science however they are able because there are sixty-five other books in the Bible that deal with more important subjects such as sin, salvation and the resurrection. But this kind of superficial reconciliation is futile. If the evolutionary naturalists are right about creation, the Bible has it wrong from the first verse to the last and is just as wrong figuratively as it is literally.

Third, Christians often think the controversy is primarily a dispute about scientific facts, and so they become trapped into arguing scientific details rather than concentrating on the fundamental assumptions that generate the evolutionary story. They ought to be asking first whether we were created by a supernatural being who cares about what we do, but instead they lose their way in technical debates over radiometric dating or geological strata.

To put it simply, Christians have been losing because they have not found the best way to state the question. They have chosen either to yield too much or to do battle on ground that favors the agnostics and religious liberals, and therefore they are always on the defensive. If they had the necessary insight, they could take the offensive. To turn a loser into a winner, they need to start with another part of Scripture.

In the Beginning Was the Word

The most important Scripture about creation teaches us not about the historical details but about the meaning of creation. Let us begin with just the first four verses of the first chapter of John:

In the beginning was the Word, and the Word was with God, and
the Word was God. He was in the beginning with God. All things
came into being through him, and without him not one thing came
into being. What has come into being in him was life, and the life
was the light of all people.

"In the beginning was the Word." Is that true or false? Is it fact
or pious platitude? I find that many intelligent people, even
devout Christians, are amazed to be asked such a question. They
have been taught to assume that "in the beginning was the Word"
belongs to the category of religion, and so it is a kind of noncog-
nitive utterance to which evaluative terms like *true* and *false* do not
apply.

Persons who have been indoctrinated in naturalistic metaphysics might begin a chapel service with the opening verses of the
Gospel of John, but it would never occur to them to begin a biology class or a business administration class with the same words.
They assume that one way of thinking governs religious topics,
and a different way of thinking governs secular topics. That is why
knowledge and piety have been so long disjoined.

There is an unacknowledged creation story that is at the root of
all secular learning which is the precise opposite of John 1:1 in
every way. You will probably never hear this creation story told
forthrightly at Harvard or Berkeley, because to state its elements
explicitly would be to reveal that it is merely one creation story
and that it is possible to conceive of another. A foundational story
is much more powerful when it is pervasively *assumed,* so that its
elements are never evaluated and it appears to be an unavoidable
implication of reason itself. The materialist story is the foundation

of all education in all the departments at all the secular universities, but they do not spell it out. It is:

> In the beginning were the particles and the impersonal laws of
>   physics.
> And the particles somehow became complex living stuff;
> And the stuff imagined God;
> But then discovered evolution.

That is the basic story of evolutionary naturalism, or scientific materialism. There was no "Word"—no intelligence or purpose—at the beginning. Only the laws and the particles existed, and these two things plus chance had to do all the creating. Without them nothing was made that has been made. The particles combined to become complex living stuff through a process of evolution that involved only chemical combinations governed by chance and natural law. God did not create man; it is the other way around. Having evolved from animals by a mindless natural process, but not having science to tell them what had happened, primitive human beings relied on their uninformed imagination to create God.

Like man, the concept of God evolved. One influential version of the story is that primitive people imagined many gods who inhabited the various features of nature—gods of river and forest and mountain. Eventually a more advanced mythology—suitable for a patriarchal, animal-herding society—combined these deities into a single, all-powerful figure who was really only a projection of their earthly fathers. The God of Abraham, Isaac and Jacob was precisely that: the personification of a tribal ancestor. This monotheistic creation story lasted until the nineteenth century, primarily because the intellectuals who wanted to reject it lacked a viable alternative.

The discovery of evolution finally made possible the "death" of God, with Charles Darwin supplying the indispensable murder weapon. This was the theory of natural selection, which made God unnecessary as creator of the living world. The general assumption in the university world throughout the twentieth century has been that religious belief as a purely human activity may persist among educated people as long as the religious belief conforms to the naturalistic teachings of science. However, belief in a personal, supernatural creator is increasingly confined to the uneducated, and may be expected to fade away as education becomes ever more universal. Even if educated people eventually become dissatisfied with materialism, they tend to turn to some unbiblical compromise like process theology, in which God evolves with the world.

The Light That Came into the World

The gospel story says that in the living Word "was life, and the life was the light of all people." The metaphor of light is repeated several times. The light shines in the darkness, but the darkness has not understood it; the true light that gives light to every man was coming into the world. Light is something that you can see, and because there is light, you can see everything else. If you are lost in a dark cave and you see a light approaching, you know that a rescuer is approaching. But even more important, when the light appears you will be able to see where you are and how you are to proceed to safety. This is one of the most important biblical themes. If it is true that all creation was by the Word, and if this creating Word really did become flesh and dwell among men, then these facts are all-important and should illuminate everything else. If men ignore the reality of the Word and pursue instead a story based on the particles, this misguided course ought to lead them into error and confusion, back into the darkness of the cave instead of out into the light. People who start from the wrong foundation don't make just one error; they create a tower of errors.

The particles story has a parallel concept of light and darkness, but of course the concepts are reversed. According to the agnostic particles story, the light that came into the world is the light of science. The darkness that the light dispelled was the darkness of superstition, stemming from the Word story. As the Harvard geneticist Richard Lewontin states, "The primary problem [for science education] is not to provide the public with the knowledge of how far it is to the nearest star and what genes are made of. . . . Rather, the problem is to get them to reject irrational and supernatural explanations of the world, the demons that exist only in their imaginations, and to accept a social and intellectual apparatus, *science*, as the only begetter of truth." (See my *Objections Sustained* [Downers Grove, Ill.: InterVarsity Press, 1998], pp. 67-70.) In short, for Lewontin science education is all about promoting agnosticism and scientism. Public relations specialists hired by the National Academy of Science may make a show of disavowing Lewontin's assessment, but I doubt that they will be willing to repudiate it emphatically and unmistakably.

Perhaps Lewontin made his statement too candidly. A more cautious purveyor of the materialist philosophy would have said that science is *one* way of begetting truth, implying that there are other ways. But if you ask what the other ways are, you will discover that they are ways of *feeling,* not *knowing.* A scientifically educated person may have feelings of awe and wonder at the beauties of nature, and may even feel devotion to a sacred cause. But these are subjective inclinations that have no status as objective knowledge. Science is always *the* way of knowing, the only path to objective knowledge that is valid for everyone. Religious belief may continue to exist in an age of science, but it will live only in the shadows of the cave, where the light of science has not yet penetrated.

The task of modernist theology is to keep peace with science by fitting God—or something that sounds vaguely like God—into the particles story. It is not difficult to do this if you are content with superficialities. For example, God may have furnished the laws and the particles in the first place. He may have left the particles to evolve on their own after that, perhaps because he wished to leave creation free of all outside influence.

Some theistic evolutionists suppose God knew that intelligent life would eventually evolve somewhere in the universe, and that was enough to satisfy his purposes. Modernist theologians are generally content to think of religion as a purely human activity anyway, so "the stuff imagined God" is not threatening to them. On the contrary, the idea that man created God in his own image appeals to them since it implies that God can be reinvented in each generation to suit the convenience of the theologians. Hence one finds the modernist theologians embracing the particles story not with reluctance but with enthusiasm on the theory that it describes a humble God who left nature free to do its own creating.

Modernist theology is nearly as despised as creationism in the modernist university, however, because it does not lead to knowledge. Once the scientists have discovered something about how the world works, the theologians can baptize it and invent some theological principle to cover it. But the theologians never discover anything, and their activity is entirely parasitic on the light that is provided only by science. As long as this is deemed to be the case, Christian institutions will be lucky to hold on to even a marginal place in the world of education. Christian intellectuals must either find a way to escape from the mental prison they have helped to construct, or the Christian faith will die the slow intellectual death of increasing irrelevance.

The Right Questions About the Religious Foundations of Education

❶ Should a college education prepare students to understand the ultimate purpose or meaning for which life should be lived and to choose rightly from among the available possibilities? Alternatively, should this subject be left out of the curriculum on the ground that the choice among ultimate purposes involves only subjective preferences and not knowledge?

It is commonplace for contemporary scientists and philosophers to give lip service to the principle that science decides only the how questions and leaves the why questions to religion. If that were literally true, then *any* answer to the why questions would be consistent with science. In practice the epistemic authority of science is so overwhelming and the standing of theology so precarious that "outside of science" effectively means "outside of reality," and the premise that science is ill-suited to determine whether the world has a purpose is taken to entail the conclusion that the world has *no* purpose. An unknowable purpose is effectively a nonexistent purpose; how could we know of the purpose if science cannot discover it?

The concept of ultimate purpose is probably inseparable from the concept of divine revelation. That is why this chapter is titled "The *Word* of God in Education," rather than the (much more tame) "Idea of God in Education." The right question is not whether God exists but whether God has revealed the nature of the ultimate purpose of the world.

Moreover the why and how questions are not easily disentangled. The Christian answer to the "chief end of man" question proceeds from the premise that God not only exists but cares about what we do, and also that eternal life exists to be enjoyed. Many persons claiming to speak for "science" would insist vehemently that these premises are false or even absurd. According to the influential Darwinist Richard Dawkins, the universe we observe "has precisely the properties we should expect if there is, at bottom, no design, no purpose, no evil and no good, nothing but blind, pitiless indifference" (*River Out of Eden* [New York: BasicBooks, 1995], p. 133).

The academic leaders of our universities may deny that they endorse the nihilism of Richard Dawkins, but it may seem that they *do* endorse it implicitly if they treat the question of right choice of the meaning of life as meaningless. Scientific materialists generally concede that individuals may choose a meaning of life for themselves, but they think of this process as inventing a meaning rather than discovering a true meaning that would exist whether they discovered it or not, in the sense that scientists may discover a new truth about the physical world, such as the speed of light. In the latter case the true figure was there to be discovered, even when no one knew what it was, and therefore scientists did not invent the generally accepted figure but discovered it.

The same logic does not necessarily apply to everything that scientists claim to have discovered. When Richard Dawkins announces confidently that materialism is true, this may be comparable to Darwin's belief that men are more intelligent than women and Europeans more intelligent than Asians or Africans— a cultural prejudice rather than a scientific theory. The Santorum Amendment discussed in chapter one was designed to make it possible to make this type of distinction in public education, and the present discussion takes the same subject into higher education. One of the right questions to ask is why the scientific and educational authorities are so fearful of what may happen if the public is encouraged to learn to distinguish between the data or testable hypotheses of science on the one hand, and religious or philosophical ideas for which scientific authority is claimed on the other.

Os Guinness provides a brief guide to the search for the meaning of life in his book *The Long Journey Home*. To illustrate what is missing from our modernist education, Guinness relates an anecdote first told by the economist E. F. Schumacher. Schumacher was sightseeing in the beautiful Russian city of St. Petersburg, then

known as Leningrad, at a time in its history when it was languish-
ing under communist rule. He realized that the map he was pains-
takingly following did not correspond to what he was seeing.
Right before him were several huge Russian Orthodox churches
with their distinctive golden onion domes. Schumacher asked the
official tour guide why the churches were not on the map. "That's
simple," the guide helpfully replied, "we don't show churches on
our maps."

Schumacher realized that the incident could stand as a parable
of his own education. It occurred to him, as he later wrote in *Guide
for the Perplexed*, that this was not the first time he had been given
a map that failed to show things he could see right in front of his
eyes. "All through school and university I had been given maps
and knowledge on which there was hardly a trace of the things
that I most cared about and that seemed to me of the greatest
importance to the conduct of my life." (Guinness explains that
Schumacher meant that the mental maps which are supplied to a
European intellectual even in noncommunist countries "gave no
place to the faith that was so vital to him.") Every Christian who
has been to a modern American university will see the point.

To pursue Schumacher's parable a bit further, we can imagine
how the Soviet authorities might respond if they had received
complaints from visitors too numerous and influential to ignore
that the maps were inadequate. They would probably have produced another map, available only in stores catering to foreigners,
which included the churches—classified as buildings of historical
interest. They could then say in good faith that "the churches are
on our maps now," but the maps would show them not as places

of current worship but as museums to a superseded faith. Perhaps our own intellectual authorities do something of the same nature when they cover materialism with the authority of "science" and marginalize theism as "religion." The effect is much the same as if they were to label materialism as "modern knowledge" and theism as "premodern superstition." Should some more evenhanded terminology be employed?

The officially designated place of worship in the Soviet Union, not (of course) under that name, is the tomb of Lenin in Moscow. When the governing authority declares the traditional religion irrelevant to modern life, it leaves a spiritual vacuum which attracts some new ideology to move into the vacancy left by the departure of the Transcendent. The sepulchre of the dead tyrant as a shrine for worship is a thoroughly un-Marxist phenomenon, but something has to stand as the symbol of the ultimate purpose of everything else. If Lenin's tomb were to be removed, then something would probably have to replace it, with incalculable consequences.

We may wonder whether contemporary America is altogether different. I leave it to the reader to imagine what realignment of the monuments in Washington, D.C., may someday be proposed. As for the monuments of faith in New York City, that is a subject to which I shall return in chapter five.

To pursue the map parable still further, suppose (counterfactually) that Schumacher's great-great-grandfather had toured the great Russian cities in 1900. He admires the great Orthodox churches but also notices a well-attended Protestant church, as well as a mosque and an apparent church building with a sign

labeling it the "Church of Reason," where Unitarian socialists meet
for discussions of political theory. "Why aren't those other
churches on the map as well?" he asks the tsarist officials.

"We do not consider those places to be genuine churches," they
reply, "but meeting places for infidels. We would have the police
close them down and arrest the ringleaders, but that would only
make martyrs and cause more problems than it would solve. We
try to take as little notice of them as possible, because there are
many impressionable young people in our Orthodox Church,
especially among university students, and they are drawn to these
houses of heresy and are frequently seduced by the insidious arguments they hear inside them. The best we can do is try to preserve
these immature minds from temptation and hope they don't discover how to find the false churches for as long as possible."

The hypothetical Schumacher ancestor would surely conclude
that the Russian Orthodox Church is on its way to a crisis. For a
ruling creed to depend for its survival on keeping its followers
from exploring the alternatives is a losing strategy in the long run,
especially when opportunities for learning are growing and the
ruling power is afraid of public opinion, and thus unwilling to use
all the force available to it.

This dilemma is also characteristic of the large American Christian subculture. If Christian parents send their youth to Christian
schools mainly to put off the evil day when they will encounter the
full seductive power of secular culture, then they are at most
delaying the inevitable apostasy, and they may not succeed in
delaying it very much. What they need to be doing is teaching the
students about the bad ideas so they can evaluate them rationally.

(The likelihood that this approach will be successful depends on whether the ideas really are bad.) On the other hand, scientific materialists may also merely be delaying the inevitable if they rely on their control over the textbooks and the mainstream media to discourage inquisitive young people from exploring alternative ways of thought. Such a strategy is particularly shortsighted in a time when new forms of communication and schooling are increasingly important.

❷ Are certain a priori commitments indispensable as a basis for the rational dialogue and mutual tolerance that are the defining characteristics of liberal education? What are those commitments, and what is the underlying basis for them?

Secular intellectuals tend to be highly critical of Christian institutions that require faculty to affirm their adherence to the fundamental doctrines of the sponsoring church, such as the authority of the Bible and the physical resurrection of Jesus. These are a priori commitments, meaning that they are not subject to continuing reexamination in the light of new evidence or changes in the intellectual climate. Secularists say that mandatory religious commitments are inconsistent with academic freedom. Do they object to a priori commitments in principle, or merely to the religious character of the commitments at the Christian colleges? What about an a priori commitment to academic freedom or to the existence of crosscultural, objectively measurable standards of intellectual or artistic merit? What worldview assumptions would justify such a commitment?

To understand the problem, imagine a course in literature at one of our best universities. The instructor (an assistant professor who hopes for promotion to tenured rank in a year or two) prescribes the reading list and hence sets the agenda for classroom discussion, but thereafter the discussion itself proceeds on the premise of social and intellectual equality. Students do not hesitate to challenge statements made in the assigned texts or by the instructor. Now assume that three students, who claim to represent many others, take this dialogue a step further. The first student plans to major in ethnic studies, the second in women's studies and the third in queer theory. The three have many points of disagreement, but for the present purpose they have united to draft a joint statement, which they have titled "A Syllabus for Justice." Following is a paraphrase of their statement, which they read aloud in class to the young instructor (Assistant Professor Robert Elegant) in a polite but insistent tone of voice.

> Bob, the reading list in this course shows an unacceptable degree of implicit racism, sexism and homophobia. It is packed with Europeans, mostly from privileged backgrounds, and the authors are all either male, heterosexual or both. This is a biased selection, and it needs to be rectified. To demonstrate that you are negotiating with us in good faith, we demand that you delete these three names: Dante, Shakespeare and Jane Austen. That will still leave mostly straight Europeans on the list. And the replacements should represent (1) oppressed racial minorities, (2) women who can eloquently express their anger at the victimization they have suffered from a patriarchal society, rather than women who are described as dutifully seeking marriages with husbands who will further oppress them, and (3) gays and lesbians who can critique the aptly named "straight jacket" that is hegemonic throughout our so-called

society. We like you, Bob, so we want to give you every chance to correct your mistakes for your own sake. You know that the standards for faculty promotions and tenure reviews that we negotiated last year specify a "commitment to diversity in every aspect of university life". as a first priority and provide that written student evaluations be considered in the promotion process.

There is one other thing, Bob. The standards say that it is the instructor's responsibility to address promptly any complaints about classroom remarks by any person which are or could be offensive to any member of any group which is underrepresented in the university, or which has suffered from discrimination. You haven't said anything all that bad yourself yet, Bob, but you laughed at some offensive jokes and didn't do anything when our class primitive complained that "chicks run everything these days, it seems." We think you ought to read that standard aloud to the class again, and make sure you speak up when some right-winger shows his insensitivity. You can pick the three replacement authors from this list of approved choices we've prepared. Think it over, Bob, and do what you think is right. We'll see you at your tenure hearing after you complete the prescribed sensitivity training.

At the next class, Professor Elegant announced that he had accepted all the demands, and he thanked the three student leaders profusely "for giving me that much-appreciated guidance." Would you say that this hypothetical scenario is altogether unrealistic, or is it merely an illustration of trends that are already visible in our contemporary universities? Do our universities have sufficiently firm commitments to traditional liberal academic values that a drama of this kind could not take place? What are those commitments?

The preceding hypothetical case is intended to reflect a possible outcome of the deterioration of the university's commitment to the traditional values of post-Enlightenment liberal education as awareness grows that there is no longer any universally recognized grounding for those commitments. Values may linger for a time without any foundation, like a house whose supporting timbers are being devoured by termites, but they collapse when the winds of change blow strongly enough. Our greatest universities redirected all their resources to support the war effort in 1941-1945. Why should they not give up some outdated ideas to support today's great campaigns for diversity and social justice?

❸ What distinctive contribution to college or university education can Christian educators or campus parachurch workers make? To make that contribution most effectively, should they concede that Christian principles are valid only for Christians, or should they proceed on the assumption that the most basic Christian doctrines are true for believers and unbelievers alike?

Some secular professors are openly contemptuous of Christian faith and seek opportunities to embarrass Christian students. More commonly, even agnostic professors are sympathetic to sincere faith if it is relegated to private worship or to nonclassroom activities like Bible study groups or volunteer services. Professors may even encourage these activities on the ground that they are more conducive to a sound academic environment than various other things the students may be doing. However, stern disapproval is likely to greet any Christian student or professor who assumes too visible a profile (hence the reluctance of most Christian professors to identify themselves publicly as such). The most important restrictions are that Christians must not aspire to change the naturalistic worldview that governs all academic activity, and above all, they must not identify themselves with "fundamentalism" by criticizing the theory of evolution.

By and large, academic Christians comply with these restrictions because they half believe that they are justified. Christians in their most confident mood believe that Christianity is True (the initial capital letter signifying a universal truth on the level of a scientific fact), and Christians in their most defensive mood think that their faith is a benefit to them that needs to be brought up to date and protected from "fundamentalists," and that must avoid at all costs the one unforgivable sin in the postmodern university, the sin of intolerance. We thus have a clash of half-believers. The Christians half believe in their own creed, and the secular academics half believe in the values of Enlightenment rationalism, including academic freedom and objective standards of merit. The only true believers, paradoxically, are the apostles of diversity, multiculturalism and epistemological relativism. That is why they have the upper hand for the time being. Christians can play a decisive role in resolving this impasse, but only if they summon the nerve and the intellectual quality to affirm without embarrassment that John 1:1-14 is really True. Eventually even the secular professors will realize that the values of Enlightenment rationalism and intellectual freedom were founded on the Word.

THREE

The First Catastrophe

UNARMED AMONG
THE DRAGONS OF THE MIND

Just Before the Event

As I passed my sixty-first birthday in July 2001, my life seemed
nicely in order and likely to continue that way. I was twenty-five
pounds overweight with moderately elevated blood pressure, but
I considered these conditions nearly normal for a man of my age
and profession. I suppose I assumed that the good health I had
always enjoyed would continue indefinitely. I was very happily
married and in a busy, comfortable retirement from a career as a
law professor. I was relaxing in a rented beach house with friends
and their young children. What could go wrong in such a stress-
free setting?

Although retired from formal university duties, I was in no
sense "on the shelf." On the contrary, my work as an author and
traveling lecturer was far more absorbing than anything I had
done before the pivotal year 1988, when I first explored the gap-

ing logical flaw in Darwinism. With the first publication of *Darwin on Trial* in 1991 I assumed the leadership of a tiny group of scholars sometimes called the Intelligent Design Movement, with a strategy we called the Wedge (explained in the introduction to my book *The Wedge of Truth*). Our bold claim was that scientific evidence, when evaluated without an overwhelming bias toward materialism, does not support the Darwinian creation story that has effectively become a state-supported religion in modernist culture. On the contrary, the evidence actually supports the supposedly discredited view that an intelligent designer outside of nature had to be involved in biological creation. Our major problem was not finding the evidence but getting our argument past the man-made philosophical barrier embedded in the very definition of *science* that forbids the consideration of evidence that may point to the role of an intelligent cause in biological creation. Nonetheless the evidence is there, and we needed only a fair opportunity to make our case.

At first most university people (including Christians) assumed that our project was as doomed to failure as Satan's rebellion against God in *Paradise Lost*, science being about as powerful in our world as God was in Milton's. I disagreed because I was convinced that the cultural power of Darwinism rested not on genuine empirical testing but on an audacious bluff backed by intimidation. Darwinists had imposed a philosophical straitjacket on science. All we needed to do was to establish a distinction between naturalism/materialism as a philosophy and empirical testing as a methodology. Once that distinction was recognized as the premise for further discussion, then the power of logic itself, like the pressure exerted by freezing water confined in a cracked rock, would carry our argument the rest of the way.

The most potent bait which modern ideologists have employed to disarm our intellectual wariness is to appeal to our vanity, or to our fear of ridicule. Freud, for example, promised his disciples that they would gain a profound understanding of why humans behave as they do, giving them a choice of either becoming a master over the forces of the unconscious through psychoanalysis or being the puppet of those same forces and of the people who *do* understand them. Along the same lines, homosexual activists won an overwhelming propaganda victory when the media began using the term *homophobia,* thus implicitly characterizing opposition to the gay rights political agenda as a form of mental illness, possibly linked to fear (phobia) of one's own homosexual inclinations. Once a term of abuse is established in the culture, it can be used to separate dangerous critics, who reject the ideological program in principle, from mild or apologetic critics who accept the philosophical essence of the program in order to avoid appearing to be ignorant or irrational. The former are anathematized, while the latter are shown to be afraid to follow the logical implications of what they have already conceded. Richard Dawkins famously wrote that

> it is absolutely safe to say that if you meet somebody who claims not to believe in evolution, that person is ignorant, stupid or insane (or wicked, but I'd rather not consider that). ("Ignorance Is No Crime," *Free Inquiry* 21, no. 3 [2001])

The characteristic Dawkins strategy of intellectual intimidation reaches its peak in the implication that there are no genuine skeptics, only poseurs who pretend not to believe. The trick is to induce the skeptic to imagine that he can avoid condemnation by saying he accepts "evolution" but has some doubts about the reigning neo-Darwinian theory. Of course, Dawkins takes advantage of the concession by underlining the illogic of accepting the principle while balking at the necessary implications of the principle.

Much the same treatment greets the hapless theistic evolutionist who accepts Darwinism as science but tries to hold on to a belief in the God of the Bible. Materialists can persuasively argue that the same logic (epistemic naturalism) that leads to Darwinism also leads to the inference that God must be merely a projection of the human mind. Why not accept the logical conclusion if you accept the premise? What good is God if he never does anything we can detect?

Dawkins tried a variant of this "fatal concession" ploy on me in an e-mail conversation by demanding to know if I would admit that humans and lobsters share a common ancestor. If I had agreed to such a fantastic proposition (the supposed "fact" of evolution), I would have left myself with no logical basis for doubting any other Darwinian claim, and Dawkins would have had grounds to insinuate that I must be only pretending to disbelieve.

Dawkins had ready a series of follow-up questions designed to tighten the noose, but I changed the subject, asking: "On what basis are you so confident that the hypothetical common ancestor of lobsters and humans is not merely an artifact of evolutionary theory but actually lived on the earth? My understanding is that your confidence is founded on philosophy, specifically on your belief in materialism and reductionism. That is what permits you to proclaim 'Universal Darwinism,' that is, that something like Darwinian evolution must be the explanation for the existence of complex life even on distant planets where we can make no observations. Am I correct, or do you have scientific evidence stemming from your specialized knowledge as a zoologist that ought to convince someone who does not already share your belief that the existence of this ancestor is a philosophical necessity?"

Dawkins responded that "the reason we know for certain we are all related, including bacteria, is the universality of the genetic code and other biochemical fundamentals. Philosophical commitment to materialism and reductionism is true, but I would prefer to characterize it as philosophical commitment to real explanation as opposed to complete lack of explanation, which is what you espouse."

I knew then that I had turned the tables on Dawkins and induced *him* to accept a fatal premise that must undermine his position in any extended public debate. That "universal genetic code" is not truly universal, but the more important point is that biochemical similarities, like the musical similarities in Beethoven's symphonies, may be evidence of a common designer rather than a common physical ancestor. By appealing to the philosophical question of what constitutes a real explanation, Dawkins had conceded that the fundamental question was outside the professional domain of biology. Of course, materialist reductionists want a reductionist explanation of everything, but that is merely a subjective preference with which neither philosophers nor citizens in general have any obligation to agree. With the issue framed that way, the Wedge movement needed only to bring the true issues into the public consciousness to set the stage for a rout.

Our aim from the start was to gain serious attention on the public stage as a scientific movement, thus avoiding the instant dismissal that awaits any hypothesis labeled as religion. I had defined success in this first phase as the appearance in the *New York Times* (or a similarly influential publication) of an article about us, not necessarily favorable, written by a science reporter rather than a religion reporter. The requisite story appeared on April 8, 2001, and not only was it written respectfully by a science writer, but it was on the front page of the Sunday edition, the best conceivable place to serve our purpose.

That success came on top of others, including the passage by the United States Senate of the Santorum Amendment, described in chapter one. It now seemed certain that we were going to get our hearing before the American public, an audience that would never agree to the Darwinist demand that they define rationality and materialism as virtually the same thing. We were going to win the coming debate not because we were more skillful debaters than the Darwinists but because we were persuading the world to ask the right question. Did the scientific evidence really support the philosophical conclusion (in a word, *naturalism*) that the Darwinists wished us to adopt, or could naturalism as a worldview survive only as long as dogmatic philosophical barriers protected it from the evidence that points to a designer? The Darwinists could keep the right question off the table only if they could keep the debate confined to the professional scientific community, where naturalistic rules of reasoning are strictly enforced. We had already escaped from that confinement.

My Worst Fear

After years of study and debate I knew all the Darwinian tricks and was confident that the truth would prevail if the right question were fairly debated in an unbiased forum. As I went to bed for a nap after lunch on Friday, July 13, 2001, I was full of faith in the logic of our argument. But there was one thing I hadn't anticipated. While I tried to sleep, a clot clogged the artery that had been carrying blood to the right side of my brain. When I got up, my wife, Kathie, saw that something was wrong, and soon I was in an ambulance and then in a hospital room, with no feeling or control on the left side of my body. My left arm was an unmanageable claw, and I was virtually unaware of anything to my left. (A right-brain stroke affects the *left* side of the body as well as general functions, such as the ability to organize information.) Even familiar faces looked different, and I was beset by confusion and depression.

Of all the bad things that might have happened to me, brain damage was the one I had feared most. Death seemed almost mild in comparison, with the shame of helplessness and the dread that my loved ones would remember me not as a source of help and wisdom but as a mental and physical cripple who had burdened their lives during his last years. In my worst moments I found myself wishing that we had doctors like people say they have in Holland, who give a painless death to patients whom they judge to have become burdensome. That was a foolish thought, of course, and it was not the last foolish thought I was to have. In those early days of stroke recovery, my ever-present companions were the "dragons of the mind," exaggerated terrors that had some basis in reality but that lost their potency when fought with the spiritual weapons provided by faith.

Now my worst fear seemed a present reality, but my hospital room was also filled with loving friends praying for and with me. As we prayed our friend Kate sang a simple hymn. I had often been thrilled to hear Kate's rich, trained voice, but this time it was the words that pierced the depth of my soul: "On Christ the solid rock I stand; all other ground is sinking sand." I could think of nothing but the man described in the Sermon on the Mount (Matthew 7:24), who built a house on a foundation of sand. When the winds and the floods came, the house fell with a mighty crash. Suppose, however, that the foolish man was fortunate, and the bad weather merely damaged his house without utterly destroying it. In that case he should be thankful for the damage and the fright, for these apparent calamities, terrible at the time, have taught him that he must rebuild on a more solid foundation and thus may have saved him from something much worse.

As I listened I told myself, *I am that foolish man.* I had been taught something about the difference between solid rock and shifting sand, but I did not sufficiently heed the teaching. I built a house, and in some respects it was a very good house, but it was not thoroughly anchored in the rock. I knew the importance of asking the right questions, such as "How solid is my foundation?" Too often, however, I had been distracted by the wrong questions, such as "How many rooms should I have?" Or "How can I make the house look impressive so the neighbors will admire it?" The storm came and shook the foundation. Providentially, my house was only damaged and not destroyed, and I had a scare that taught me a lesson I would not have learned otherwise. Am I asking the right questions? Are you? That is what any education worthy of the name ought to teach us to do, but too often our formal education neglects the most important questions, or even conceals them, and so we have to learn the most important lessons through experience, often costly experience.

Kate's song was asking the right question! What *was* the solid rock on which I stood? I had always prided myself on being self-reliant, and my brain was what I had relied on. Now the self with its brain was exposed as the shaky instrument it had always been. I was a Christian, even an ardent one after my worldly fashion, but now all the smoke was blown away and I saw Truth close up. I knew myself to be not so much a believer in Christ as a skeptic about everything else, a recovering rationalist who had lost his faith in the world's definition of reason, but who knew only the world's Jesus. That Jesus seemed too sentimental a thing to bear the full weight of a life at its most desperate moment.

A New Commitment

I had long been a searcher, but the time for searching was past. Like Don Giovanni at the opera's climactic moment, I had to decide *now* and for eternity where my hope was based, or whether I had any. I knew at least that my own brain was no solid rock. Even modern medicine, when I was faced with the uncertainties of stroke recovery and the likelihood of further strokes, appeared to be a very chancy thing. There is no cure for a stroke, only therapy and coping. I knew that my damaged neurons were gone for good. In time, with strenuous therapy, I would recover a degree of normal function. No one could say in advance how swiftly the recovery would happen or how far it would go. What I needed was the only solid rock, the real Christ, the Word made flesh. This rock had to support me not only in pursuing therapy but also in learning to live faithfully for the rest of my life with whatever disability might remain.

As Kate finished her song, I knew that I had found the solid rock and that I was already standing on it. My brothers and sisters in Christ prayed with me for a miracle of healing, and I felt the miracle beginning to happen. As I recalled it a little later, I said that "if heaven is an eternity of love, then I have had an hour of it already." That was enough miracle for the first day; I had met and vanquished the first dragon of the mind. There would be many more dragons to come, but I knew I would not face them alone or unarmed. I recalled the familiar words of the Twenty-third Psalm from the King James Bible: "Yea, though I walk through the valley of the shadow of death, I will fear no evil: for thou art with me." I told Kathie, "To me that has always been just a beautiful poem, but now I know what it means." I had walked through the valley of the shadow of death, and that psalm was now my own story. Lord, I believe; please help my unbelief! That juxtaposition is not paradoxical to those who have been there.

The Right Questions About Logic

❶ What is the ultimate premise, the beginning point from which logic should proceed?

In Greek the "Word" is the *Logos*, the root of logic. That word encompasses both the human activity of reasoning and the divine foundation from which logic must begin. Our logic cannot supply its own beginning. Logic is merely a way of reasoning correctly from premises to conclusions. The premises must come from elsewhere. Rationalism is inherently self-defeating, because the rationalist must pretend to derive his first premises by logical reasoning, which always rests on *other* premises. Empiricism faces the same dilemma when it becomes a total system because the empiricist always needs to know more than he can observe. Premise-evading philosophies like logical positivism or scientific materialism last only until the dilemma becomes too evident to be concealed, and then they wither. That is why the guardians of such systems when under pressure often become fanatics who try to impose authoritarian control. Forbidding examination of the premises is the only way they can continue to rule.

❷ Can we resolve conflicting premises by argument?

Some writers divide the field of Christian apologetics into two schools: the evidentialists and the presuppositionalists. When I am asked to which camp I belong, I reply that the distinction is unhelpful in my work. My problem is not with presuppositions as such, but with *concealed* presuppositions, which come disguised as facts. When a dogmatic Darwinist like Richard Dawkins admits that his belief is ultimately based on philosophy, he undercuts his own authority. In principle he could still hold to materialism as an ultimate premise even if the rest of the world were to discard Darwinism as a failed theory, but he would hold on despairingly, and

I think he would soon let go.

Ultimate premises do not yield to argument or evidence, but a premise that appears to be ultimate may turn out not to be ultimate after all. I think it would be so with Dawkins. But if anything I may say could move a materialist to choose a better ultimate premise, it would probably not be my arguments but my story of what happened to me in that hospital room and to countless others in their time of ordeal. Christ is a rock to which one can cling in the valley of the shadow of death, or even when the world mocks and humiliates Christ. That is the story of what happened to that tiny, confused band of disciples after the resurrection. I do not think that any worldly faith or man-made god provides anything comparable.

Note that I am writing about the ultimate *premise*, or faith commitment, from which life and logic should proceed. I am therefore not writing about some doctrine that requires proof. Trying to prove an ultimate premise is an absurdity. Such an attempt at proof would have to proceed from something else that is both more fundamental and more certainly true than "in the beginning was the Word" and "the Word became flesh and dwelt among us." In that case our ultimate premise would be that something else, and in time we would learn the hard way, as we are now doing, that the something else cannot bear the load.

"God creates" and "God cares" state the premise abstractly. John 1:1-14 states it as a metanarrative, the grand story of the world. If you are a rationalist you will probably recoil at the thought of an acknowledged premise, a fundamental proposition that comes at the beginning rather than at the end of a chain of logical reasoning.

But the rationalist also has a first premise: the reliability of the autonomous mind and its powers of reasoning, powers that, according to scientific materialism, amount to nothing more than so many neurons firing in the physical brain. I wonder if anyone has ever held on to such a faith in the aftermath of a stroke.

Postmodern epistemological relativists reject all metanarratives in principle because their own metanarrative tells of independent cultures or interpretive communities who declare their independence from all universal values or standards of rationality. Enlightenment rationalists imagined that the death of God would leave human reason in command, much as naive anarchists have imagined that they could maximize freedom by abolishing government. The rationalists prepared the ground for the nihilists who came after them, and the naive anarchists only maximized the freedom of tyrants.

❸ What does it mean to believe the ultimate premise? Is there such a thing as belief without obedience? Can one believe Christ and yet hesitate to commit one's life to him?

What struck me in that hospital room was the absurdity of dithering, or of hesitating to part with something of only temporal value when one is offered something of eternal value. The call of Jesus is expressed as "follow me," not "think it over and get back to me." Of course I had thought it over, and perhaps that is why I could hear the call. But in his last moment Don Giovanni must repent or be lost because there is no more time to think it over. That last moment arrives whenever the Holy Spirit makes the sinner aware that "the time is now," even if the world's clocks and calendars show that there is plenty of time left. I have passed through the valley of the shadow of death, and I have decided for Christ at the final moment. Those who have been there know already what that experience is like. Those who have not been there must be prepared. But what happens after that peak experience? If you will stay with me I will tell you what has happened to me.

FOUR

My New Post

THE ROAD FORWARD

The Lowest Point

Probably the lowest point of my life was just following my initial hospitalization for the stroke. I was sent for a week or two to the Rounseville Convalescent Facility in Oakland, California, to await a vacancy in the nearby Kaiser Vallejo Hospital, which is famed for its neurological therapy and stroke rehabilitation programs. The limited therapy available at Rounseville was in fact just right for a first step, but I was impatient for more, and the ambience of the place depressed me. Many of the patients were elderly, and it was evident that they were never going back to a normal life.

One of the things I remember hearing around that time was that having had one stroke increases tenfold your chances of having another, a prospect that made my future seem bleak. I confronted imaginary terrors, which I began to call "dragons of the mind," every day and especially during the long nights when I lay sleepless, waiting for the morning. Despite my resolve to rest on the solid rock of God's promises, I constantly imagined the worst. I wondered if I would ever lecture again or write for publication. I even worried about money, although insurance was taking care of everything and our resources were more than adequate for our modest needs.

There were also times when the clouds of worry lifted, especially when friends dropped in to visit or Kathie appeared in the early morning with a thermos of real coffee. I needed her presence for reassurance because I was on an emotional roller coaster, jovial when things were going well and then exploding with frustration when I could not cope. This is standard behavior following a right-brain stroke, made worse by my perception of myself as the family provider on whom others depend but who imagined himself never needing to depend on others. Up to a point this determination to be self-reliant was a positive quality, but carried too far it just created an additional burden for the caregivers. We are taught to think of charity in terms of gracious giving, but I was learning that gracious receiving is sometimes the best way of giving.

I was exhilarated a week into my stay at Rounseville, when a surprise phone call told me that a place in the Vallejo Rehabilitation Facility had opened up, and that Kathie could drive me there the next day in our own car. I arrived at Vallejo in a wheelchair, eager to begin the famously demanding therapy, whereupon the staff put me to bed and then seemed to forget all about me. I was still depressed that evening when a young scientist on our Wedge team unexpectedly arrived, bringing with him the beautiful and brilliant medical student he was courting. They brought me the best gift of all, the ability to forget my stroke disability and to concentrate for an hour on the much more interesting subject of young love, encouraging them as best I could to take the next big step toward what I was sure would be a union blessed by heaven.

When I did think of myself again, the book of Job repeatedly came to mind, as if it were trying to tell me something. My modernist-educated mind had always conceived of Job as an inconclusive philosophical debate enclosed between two fabulous bookends. Like the Twenty-third Psalm, the fable made beautiful poetry, but I couldn't see how it made much sense as reality. Would God allow Satan to torment a man just to test his faith? How did it make things right for God to provide Job at the end with a *second* family, along with other possessions exceeding what he had lost? What about the innocent victims? Were they no more than possessions?

When I imagined myself as the protagonist, however, the objections faded away. Of course the book is the story of Job and not of his entire clan. It does not make sense to ask what Job's story can tell us about the meaning of all those other lives because it is not *their* story. More generally, people sometimes go to the book of Job hoping it will explain why bad things happen to good people. By that time I was indwelling the Bible sufficiently to know that this was not the right question for me to be asking. What can I know of such a universal matter, or even of people who are unqualifiedly good? That question belonged to my worldly, rationalist past. It would be more appropriate to ask, "Why did this particular bad thing happen to *me just now?*" That was the question the book of Job prodded me to ask, and I was filled with a certainty that God was answering that question even as I was asking it.

Once I focused on the right question, it seemed fitting that Satan might point to me as he had to Job and say to God, "Of course that Phillip Johnson gives praise and thanks to you; why should he not? He has always enjoyed prosperity and good health, despite not having done much either to deserve or to preserve this good fortune. Beyond health and comfort, he has been gifted with a mind that permitted him to rise to a high rank in the academic world, even while his attention was mainly elsewhere. After one marriage failed, God gave him another, better one, just as God gave Job other possessions and another family. Then in middle age he was blessed with an insight, and this answer to prayer provided the impetus for a new vocation that fully employs his gifts for a campaign that gives meaning to his life.

"His thanks to God are superficial, for in his heart he sometimes still indulges the thought that all these blessings are no more than what he deserves. He will never know who he really is unless you permit me to loose a blood clot in his carotid artery so that he learns just how insubstantial are the things on which he has based his confidence. Maybe then he will curse thee to thy face."

At that point I imagine God saying to Satan, "Behold, he is in your power, only spare his life" (Job 2:6 NASB), and I imagine my own true self assenting, saying "Yes, there is no other way for me to know myself."

If that reading of Job seems egocentric, I can only say that the biblical story of Job is both about a particular man and also about all of us. I am trying to explain what I know and how I learned it, and I learned about the meaning of my own suffering in the light of what the Bible teaches.

There is more. God helped me to ask the right question and also provided the answer I needed at the moment I began to ask. I had been wondering how I could get back to where I had been just before the day of the stroke, in possession of all my faculties and fit to direct the Wedge in the decisive moment of our struggle. At the same time I had reason to think that the decisive breakthrough had probably already been made, in which case other persons would probably have the privilege of taking the steps to follow. The closed cognitive world of evolutionary science would be split open whether or not I was the one to do it, because so many people knew by now the fatal flaw in the Darwinian logic. The intellectual tools needed to separate scientific inquiry from epistemic materialism are now widely understood, and Christians will either make use of them or they will not. Either way, I realized, the outcome would not be up to me. If intelligent Christians followed up on what the Wedge (and earlier critics) had already accomplished, then Darwinism would strangle in its own tangle of illogic. If educated Christians continued to accept docilely the understanding that naturalism and "science" (that is, knowledge) are virtually the same, then nothing human could save such a cowardly faith.

A Changed Situation

The right question was not how I could go back to where I was but how I could go forward to live rightly in the changed situation. Of course, I had no inkling of how *much* the situation was about to change. I will write of that in the next chapter. What God seemed to be telling me in the hospital was something like this: "There has been a change in plan, and you are at your new post—where you are meant to be for this part of your life. You are not to complain that you would rather be at your old post but must make the most of the opportunity before you, to take advantage of the magnificent rehabilitative services and to encourage the other patients and the therapists. The purpose of this time is not to make you again just as you were, but to make of you something better, someone more nearly fit to dwell in God's kingdom." And so it was to be.

The experts have written that stroke survivors tend to become self-centered, and it was true that my bafflement at what was happening to me sometimes made me burst with frustration, even though I knew that the therapists and visitors were just doing their best to help me. My frustration was immediately followed by repentance and a determination to encourage whomever I had just shouted at. It was as if Christ were living within me and overcoming the natural man, and I suppose that was precisely what was happening. My sinful nature was still active in the outbursts, but it was quickly overmastered by something far more powerful.

I knew already that the most powerful witness is often given by those who are suffering and struggling, and I found this to be true of me also. I remembered the life story of a brilliant young doctor, an oncologist, raised in a scientific materialist family, who came to Christ through the faith she saw in her cancer patients. I have also seen that faith in the witness of friends dying of cancer, and I knew that my own suffering, compared to theirs, was no great matter.

Those who think in worldly abstractions and want to do God's job for him often point to the suffering of the innocent as an insu-

perable barrier to faith. To those who know Jesus, the cross is just
where Christ is likeliest to be found, because the suffering of Good
Friday always precedes the joy of Easter. I do not think that I knew
Jesus at all until knew him in suffering, and so I could never wish
that suffering altogether undone if that meant that its effects would
be wiped out from my life.

The Right Questions About the Meaning of Life

❶ How do we know the main road in life from a detour?

The main road for each of us is the road God has planned, the one
that takes us through the experiences which give meaning to our
life. But the meaning as God sees it may not be the meaning as
man sees it. As I pondered the lesson of my new post, I received a
letter from a friend named Mark, a younger man with children still
at home. Mark faced highly invasive treatment for a life-threaten-
ing cancer. Of course he prayed to be delivered from suffering and
death, but he did not consider his ordeal to be meaningless. He
thought of the experiences of Joseph and of Job. When Joseph was
sold by his brothers into Egyptian slavery (and then wrongly
imprisoned because of Potiphar's wife), he must have thought he
was suffering a meaningless interruption in an otherwise produc-
tive life. Instead God was starting one of the greatest works in the
history of his people. Think what the world would have lost if Job
had not suffered and we did not have his example to learn from.
What seems at first to be a pointless detour may be revealed in the
end to be the main road home. That has been the case with my
stroke. Like Joseph in Egypt or Job in misfortune, I learned in time

that my new post was God's way of helping me toward a greater good.

❷ What is the difference between scientific healing and faith healing, and what are the roles of faith and prayer in healing?

There is a delightful joke about the scientist who kept a horseshoe nailed above his laboratory door. "Do you really believe that horseshoe brings you good luck?" asked a colleague.

"Certainly not," replied the first scientist, "but it seems to work whether you believe in it or not."

That really is the distinguishing feature of scientific medicine: it works whether you believe in it or not. The medicine or treatment cures because of its objective properties and not because of the subjective belief of the healer or the patient. A placebo may cure, and it is likely at least to make the patient feel better temporarily, but another pill with a different chemical constitution will work just as well if the patient believes in *its* curative power. No agnostic researcher would be surprised to learn that prayer has a positive effect if the patient knows about the praying and believes in its efficacy. This is the familiar power of positive thinking, which may influence the body in subtle ways, and there is nothing inherently supernatural about it. If the prayer, however, works just as well "whether you believe in it or not," then prayer (or any previously scorned alternative remedy) can in principle be incorporated into scientific medicine. Some reports suggest that this may be the case.

The *New York Times* on December 9, 2001, carried a story by science writer Jim Holt titled "Prayer Works." Researchers at

Columbia University were astonished to find that women in a Korean fertility clinic were almost twice as likely to get pregnant when, without their knowledge, total strangers in distant countries were praying for their success. According to the report, the persons praying had only pictures of the anonymous patients for whose pregnancy they were praying, and the patients knew nothing of the prayer. "So the apparent influence of prayer could not be attributed to their beliefs or expectations or to some kind of placebo effect."

Of course the statistically significant effect could also be due to chance or some subtle defect in the study's design, but this would also be a possibility with any orthodox medical treatment that produces only a statistical benefit, like the surgery that was performed on my carotid artery to reduce the likelihood of another stroke. My own reservation about the story is thus not scientific but theological. A prayer which has a reliable effect regardless of the spiritual state of the person praying or the person prayed for seems less a prayer than a magic incantation. Holt's story indicated that skeptics would continue to disbelieve in supernatural intervention on philosophical grounds regardless of the outcome of studies, thus echoing the remark of Jesus about the skeptics of his own time that "even if a man were to return from the dead, they would not believe."

For their part, believers in the supernatural efficacy of prayer would probably be more impressed with dramatic anecdotes than with double-blind scientific studies. Holt provided a terrific anecdote: "Remember way back in 1985 when Pat Robertson publicly prayed that Hurricane Gloria, which was violently working its way up the Atlantic Coast, would miss his Christian Broadcasting Network's headquarters in Virginia Beach? It did—and then made land at Fire Island, flattening the summer house of Calvin Klein." Of course a freak event does not constitute scientific evidence, but if I were Calvin Klein, I hope that the experience would prompt me to give serious thought to changing my way of life.

I have my own miracle story, not spectacular enough to make the newspapers but just as dramatic for me. The physical therapy at my renowned stroke rehabilitation hospital was called Proprioceptive Neuromuscular Facilitation (PNF), and its scientific status was uncertain. Therapists responded only vaguely when asked about controlled studies, and one told us that "we don't know how it works, but we know it does." I would never have consented to invasive treatment on such a cloudy basis, but PNF involved only exercises to build strength and balance, so I had nothing to lose.

Once committed to the therapy I became a devotee, so much so that near the end of my stay the therapists-in-training chose me to be the subject of a master class led by Sue Adler, an elderly but very fit renowned PNF trainer. She took me through a series of demanding exercises for over an hour, which I pursued as if competing for a spot in the Olympics. At last she pointed to my wife Kathie across the gymnasium and suggested calmly that I walk over to her. To this point I had taken only a few tentative steps with a walker, but now I took Sue's hand and walked confidently across the gym to Kathie. Sue then asked Kathie to put out *her* hand so I could take it and walk with her the length of the gym, which we did. Do you know the story of Jesus asking Peter to walk to him on the water? The psychological experience was exactly as if Kathie or I had been Peter, except that our faith did not falter. Was there a naturalistic explanation? Of course there was, and Sue promptly gave it to the German trainees, who (fearful of American tort liability) wondered how she had dared to take such a risk. She explained that she had watched me carefully during the exercises and (unlike the trainees) had enough experience to be confident in her judgment of my capability. Does the explanation imply that there was no miracle? Believe if you can and scoff if you must, but do not ask me to doubt. Now when I read of Jesus and Peter walking on the water, I do not believe; I *know* because I have been there.

Later I had surgery on my carotid to clean it out in order to reduce the risk of another stroke. Controlled studies showed that the surgery was effective but also that a small percentage of patients suffered a stroke on the operating table or during the preliminary arteriogram. Here I relied on science, but of course I did not read the studies myself. I relied on the skill and reputation of the surgical team.

The first surgeon I talked with had a brusque manner which did not inspire confidence, and I declined to go ahead. The second surgeon spoke to me as if to a fellow professional, and I thought, *If I must put my life in the hands of some surgeon, I want it to be this man and no other.* The anesthesiologist phoned the day before the operation and gave me his reassuring viewpoint. The next morning I took his arm and walked into the operating room as calmly as if I were just going to bed, and the next thing I knew I was laughing and joking with the nurses in the recovery room. Everything was done according to the best scientific standards, and yet this, too, was an example of faith healing. If I live to be ninety, probably years longer than I would have done without the wake-up provided by the stroke, then this too will be a product of faith—faith in the curative power of the body if we treat it as God meant for it to be treated.

③ What is the chief end of man, and why do we need to know?

The Westminster Shorter Catechism affirms that "the chief end of man is to glorify God, and to enjoy Him forever." Is there a better answer to that question? Is the question unavoidable? Our public and private educational systems generally avoid this question because they classify it as religion and therefore assume that any answer must belong to the realm of subjective preference rather than that of knowledge. There are understandable reasons for this evasion, but think what is lost in consequence! What would one of our most privileged graduates (like the young Phillip Johnson) answer is the chief end of man? Does "he who dies with the most toys" win the game of life? Is the goal an accumulation of plea-sures, knowledge, vivid experiences or worldly triumphs? As a young man I would have endorsed the last. To die a revered Supreme Court Justice or military hero who saves the nation or a giant among Nobel Prize winners—one of those must be the chief end of man, I thought. It is to glorify oneself and thus live forever in fame.

That is the goal of the immature striver, and I think there is probably something distinctively masculine about it. Women do not benefit by being taught to ape the goals of masculine immatu-rity. I had impressive academic credentials, but on the most important subject of all I was uneducated. The map of my city did not show the cathedrals. If our educational institutions cannot teach students how to find the chief end of life, then they cannot teach the one thing that gives direction to all the things that they do teach, and someone else must find a way to complete their teaching that supplies the lack. That is why I have chosen to devote my years of retirement from the university to making it possible to teach the indispensable subject that the metaphysics of modernity casts aside.

FIVE

The Second Catastrophe

THE TOTTERING TOWERS OF FAITH

Responding to Attacks

I woke up early on September 11, 2001, and booted up my computer to check the news on the Internet. I thus saw the earliest coverage of the hijacked jetliners striking the twin towers of the World Trade Center and the appalling destruction that followed. Anyone familiar with the Internet knows that hoaxes abound, and so it is wise not to repeat any sensational news until you are absolutely sure it really happened. As I paused to be sure my eyes were not deceiving me, I remember thinking, *I sure do hope that this is the mother of all Internet hoaxes.*

When the reality and extent of the devastation became clear, the following hours were largely spent wondering and worrying about what would come next. Many books will be written (and indeed already have been written) about the terrorist attack and the war that has followed. Such a narrative is not to my purpose. Rather, my goal is to describe some of the right questions that are beginning to emerge as the public has time to react to the changed situation.

The first public comment I recall hearing after the collapse of the towers was attributed to the right-wing Christian minister Jerry Falwell, who was said to attribute the tragedy to God's disgust at the wickedness of civil libertarians, Falwell's usual targets, particularly abortionists and homosexuals. This crudity was instantly condemned from every point on the political spectrum, including the religious right. However, the reaction from journalists was in many cases far more "over the top" than the original remark, with various commentators suggesting that Falwell (and perhaps all Christian fundamentalists) belonged in the same category as the Islamicist terrorists who had hijacked the airplanes. Just as Falwell had seen the disaster as an opportunity to blame his usual scapegoats, the mainstream journalists seized the opportunity to blame their own preferred scapegoats—Christian fundamentalists. It probably never occurred to them that they were doing exactly the same thing that they condemned Falwell for doing. By media convention, religious "fundamentalists" (loosely defined) are what may be called designated scapegoats who can be blamed at any time for just about anything. Homosexuals and abortion providers are in a protected category, however, and one rarely reads anything unfavorable about them in the newspapers.

From the opposite side of the Atlantic, and on the opposite side of the metaphysical spectrum from Jerry Falwell, the arch-Darwinist Richard Dawkins saw an opportunity to use the disaster as a club to berate *his* usual targets, religious people in general, especially Christians. The root cause of fanaticism, Dawkins thought, was belief in life after death, which can turn an ordinary person into a self-guided missile capable of committing some horrible act, such as the suicide attack we had just witnessed on television, in the hope of earning a reward in paradise.

Dawkins's remark was patently absurd following a century in which a materialist philosophy called Marxist-Leninism had been responsible for over 100 million deaths. Dawkins was not publicly shamed as Falwell had been because most prominent journalists share his prejudice, if in slightly milder form. My own inclination is not to emphasize the absurdity of blaming Christians for Islamist extremism but rather to focus on the one thing that Dawkins had gotten right.

It is true that a man who believes in something that is more important to him than life itself is potentially a dangerous man. He may do things that a person with more mundane purposes would never think of doing. This is true of secular as well as religious faiths. Consider, for example, the American Revolutionary War patriot Nathan Hale, who famously regretted that he had but one life to give for his country. Such a person may be capable of a suicide attack, given a sufficiently worthy end. (I would like to ask Dawkins if *he* may be capable of sacrificing his own life in an act of murderous violence if he were convinced that such an extreme measure was necessary to save science from being taken over by religious fundamentalists.) People who care for nothing beyond their own comfort are safer, although a whole lot less inspiring, than people who are capable of risking their lives. Would we therefore wish that the world were rid of all causes and purposes that are larger than life so we could rely on people to behave more like sheep, content to graze in comfortable pastures? No.

The right conclusion to draw from the terrorist attack is not that no one should have a cause worth dying for, but rather that it is of great importance that such highly motivated persons be dedicated to a good cause rather than an evil one. This conclusion assumes that we have a standard capable of distinguishing good from evil, and this may be in doubt in an era of moral relativism when those for whom the supreme value is "tolerance" consider it more reprehensible to name evil than to do evil. If science is our only source of knowledge, and science gives us knowledge only of fact and not of value, then distinguishing between good and evil can only be a matter of arbitrary preference. Multitudes of young people have drawn precisely that conclusion, as their education has encouraged them to do.

Dawkins caricatured religious faith as if it were another kind of technology like hypnosis, useful for manipulating people. The terrorists may have believed something similar. They believed that their faith and determination, compared with the spiritual laziness and moral degeneracy that they attributed to their enemies, was great enough to overcome the immense material and technological superiority of the nation they were attacking. In a limited sense, they accomplished their objective. Whatever we may say about the evil of mass murder, and whatever may turn out to be its lasting effect (beyond the destruction of the Taliban government in Afghanistan), the attack was a brilliant tactical success by the terrorists, employing some of their enemy's most technologically advanced equipment to achieve a spectacularly destructive effect that the victims would never have imagined possible. The terrorists could never have built a jetliner, but they were skilled and ruthless at the centuries-old practice of piracy.

The first lesson to be drawn from this catastrophe is that American and European intellectuals have been very foolish to treat religious belief with patronizing disdain, as a remnant of premodernist thought that is doomed to fade in importance as mankind becomes more technologically advanced. I hope we will hear no more of that complacent illusion. The beliefs that the terrorists held, however misguided or evil, were powerful enough to make them very dangerous.

One of the results of the terrorist attack will surely be a vastly increased interest in Islam in particular and religious faith in general. This is not a subject which even a technologically advanced and wealthy nation can afford any longer to ignore. People who believe in things that rationalists consider impossible may also be able to *do* things that rationalists consider impossible. If faith made the terrorists dangerous, then faith is something we had better learn to understand in order to employ it for good purposes.

There is another side to the point Dawkins was trying to make. A faith larger than life can inspire murderous fanaticism if it is misdirected, but faith can also produce the courage needed to overcome murderous fanaticism. There is a popular saying that all that is necessary for evil to triumph is that good men do nothing. Evil may triumph if persons bent on evil have great determination and ability, and it may also triumph if potentially good people are lazy, self-centered and unwilling to risk their lives even for a noble cause.

The terrorists of September 11 thought of America much as Hitler thought of Britain and America in 1939. Ruthless fanatics act boldly, and even recklessly, because they are blind to the dormant spiritual resources possessed by a free people, and because they think their enemies are too luxury-loving and timid to fight even for their lives. The passenger heroes of flight 93, who fought the terrorists, causing them to crash their hijacked airplane in a rural location, instantly provided a dramatic demonstration that the terrorists were dead wrong about America, however right they may have been about some Americans.

In the coming years Americans will be concerned not with how to do away with faith but with how to encourage the self-sacrificing heroism demonstrated by New York City police and firefighters, U.S. military personnel in Afghanistan and many civilians. I have not heard anybody say that we need more nihilist literary theorists or more liberal clergy who preach moral equivalence. We certainly do not need more home environments or educational systems of the kind that molded the outlook of the infamous American Taliban John Walker Lindh. Lindh was willing to closely associate himself with those who would commit appalling crimes and folly, but in some respects he seems almost normal for an American youth of his time and place.

Lindh began his journey to radical Islam and then to fighting against his own country after reading *The Autobiography of Malcolm X,* a book assigned and even venerated throughout our multiculturalist educational system. His parents encouraged him, as many do, to experiment with various creeds and ways of life until he found one that suited him.

Several months *after* the terrorist attack, I saw newspaper reports of public schools that were presenting Islam to students in a highly favorable light, although these same schools would never have dared to present anything favorable about Christianity. Islam fits within the reigning ideology of multicultural diversity, whereas Christianity is associated in the public school educators' mindset with the sort of bias from which multiculturalism is supposed to help students escape. It is no wonder that such a mixed-up culture produces extreme cases like Lindh and a great many more students who get the idea that the public schools are trying to teach them that Islam is good and Christianity is bad. Why else would the former be welcome in the schools and the latter rigorously, even fanatically, excluded? Parental efforts to instill a strong faith in children may sometimes go overboard, but the case of the American Taliban demonstrates the danger of leaving curious young people with a spiritual vacuum where faith ought to be, a vacuum available to be filled by any plausible rogue or fanatic who finds it.

Real Power

Shortly after September 11, the *New York Times* published an editorial commenting that the terrorists chose the towers of the World Trade Center as the most visible symbols of America's wealth and power. I picked up this thought in an editorial that was broadcast on Christian radio stations nationwide: If the terrorists thought that the World Trade Center towers represented America's real power, they were making the same mistake that the Japanese militarists had made sixty years previously when *they* thought that the battleships at anchor in Pearl Harbor represented America's might.

It is said that the Japanese admiral remarked after the attack, "I fear we have only awakened a sleeping giant." He was right. The Pearl Harbor attack was a brilliant tactical success for the Japanese navy and a strategic disaster for both imperial Japan and Nazi Germany. I predicted that the same would be true for the Islamist terrorists. The real power of America, I said, is not material, but spiritual; it is in the faith and dedication to freedom of our people.

Immediately after recording these words, I found myself wondering whether I had spoken the plain truth, unvarnished by wishful thinking. Despite the heroism of some, the America of 2001 was not the America of 1941. The years of comfort and safety had taken their toll, with the result that philosophies of hedonism and nihilism had become dominant among the sheltered intellectuals in our universities and cultural centers. A similar demoralization was evident in Britain in the 1930s before Winston Churchill rallied his nation just in time for its finest hour. The contemporary equivalent of the appeasement mentality which had sapped Britain's strength was a philosophy of moral equivalence which, in the name of "tolerance," forbade recognizing any distinction between good and evil.

The pronouncements of some of our more spiritually flabby clergy and intellectuals after September 11 left me with the impression that they considered the terrorists to have been at least partly justified. These "nattering nabobs of negativism," as a politician of the 1970s had alliteratively termed the defeatists of his time, did not exactly approve of the terrorism, but they disapproved of any conceivably effective measures for dealing with the perpetrators. What had once been called anti-anti-communism lived on as anti-anti-terrorism. The courageous and effective conduct of the war in Afghanistan by American military personnel under the leadership of President Bush was inspiring, but some parts of American culture were an asset only to the enemies of freedom. Fashionable public intellectuals and elite journalists were mostly clueless in responding to the changed situation after September 11, probably because their ideologically confined education and limited experience with people who do not think exactly as they do had left them incapable of understanding that the situation really had changed.

All these people could do was to replay the scripts they already knew: Vietnam, civil rights and Watergate. In each of these crises the print and broadcast media had played a dominant role. In the Vietnam War, the media pundits had discredited America's military and political leadership; in the civil rights campaigns they had enjoyed the satisfaction of championing a noble cause to overwhelming triumph; and in the Watergate scandal they had even driven a president whom they hated from office. It is not surprising, then, that the most powerful journalists seemed eager to force the events of 2001 into molds that earlier media pundits had constructed for the very different events of the 1970s. Thus the pundits warned that any war in Afghanistan would result in a deadlocked "quagmire" in which American air power would be ineffective. The reporters relentlessly pursued factoids that could be made to fit into the "officials abuse power" or "minorities suffer discrimination" templates.

Fortunately new forms of journalism were emerging, especially on radio and the Internet, and for once the media elites were subjected to the kind of critical analysis that they had long assumed would be applied only to others. If Americans have learned to be skeptical of the heavily biased reporting that has dominated both the electronic and print media since 1960, the terrorists of September 11 will have given us an unintended benefit to weigh against the evil they have done. I am hopeful that talented writers and speakers will come forward now to raise the important questions that have been kept from public view by the media monopolies. Probably only a financial disaster will ever motivate the owners of the elite media to awake to reality, and the disaster will be slow in coming as long as advertisers are selling their products. The best we can hope for in the short run is that there will be ample alternative sources of information.

The Right Questions About Religion and Tolerance in a Pluralistic Society

❶ What is the appropriate understanding of religion in a pluralistic nation like the United States, where substantial numbers of Christians, agnostics, religious Jews and Muslims all need to live together in peace?

Shortly after the September 11 attack, a *New York Times* columnist wrote that the war against terrorism should be a war against what he called "religious totalitarianism," meaning the view that only one religion is true and all the others are therefore false, to the extent that they contradict the true religion. Superficially that may seem like the "tolerant" position, but in fact it is an attempt to absolutize one religious position—agnosticism—in order to justify relativizing all the others. The best way to state the substantive point at issue is to ask, "What is the correct metaphysical viewpoint, that is, the correct description of 'how things really are,' against which all claims of religious truth or exclusiveness should be evaluated?"

For most university-educated men and women of the twentieth century, the assumed "one true metaphysic" will almost certainly be scientific naturalism or, to use a simpler but loaded term, *modernism*. Under whatever name, the naturalistic worldview assumes that nature is a closed world of material causes and effects, which we understand through scientific investigation, and that supernatural interventions into the natural order have never occurred. Influential opinion makers, like that *New York Times* columnist, make a show of condemning claims of religious exclusiveness only because they assume a religious exclusiveness of a different kind. If modernism (naturalism) is True (the initial capital letter signifying that the claim is one of objective or universal truth), then Jesus did not rise from the tomb, and Muhammad did not receive any portion of the Qur'an directly from Allah. To modernists, Christianity and Islam are equally true because they are equally false, or at least their incorrigibly supernaturalist elements are false. If modernism is the one true religious worldview, then the other religions, insofar as they are inconsistent with modernism, must be false. In my experience most university-educated people assume exactly that, without feeling it necessary to give the matter much thought. That is what their minds have been trained to do.

Most modernists bristle at the suggestion that modernism is a religion or even a metaphysical viewpoint because that would imply that modernism is merely one of the possible ways of thinking about the world rather than the only acceptable way for educated people to think. *Religion* is a pejorative term in modernist metaphysics, connoting fantasy or wishful thinking, and usually inclining toward intolerance or even oppression. To its faithful adherents modernism is not a religion or an optional philosophy but "the way we think today"—"we" meaning all the people whose opinions count. The possibility that modernism could be shown to be false or replaced peacefully by some more persuasive alternative does not occur to them. Modernism is a dominant religious worldview—one which seems so obviously correct that it does not need to be justified. It is just "what everybody knows." To classify naturalism as one of several religious worldviews would make its crucial assumptions visible, so that they would have to be defended just as the assumptions underlying other religious worldviews have to be defended. The modernist hegemony depends on preventing that situation from arising.

Modernists cannot afford to have their assumptions exposed for analysis because everybody *doesn't* know that naturalism is true—not even every acclaimed scholar or scientist. The unbelievers (in modernism) have been intimidated and marginalized throughout the twentieth century because cognitive elites have employed enormously powerful propaganda to convince people, especially students, that the truth of naturalism has been verified by science, the same science that gives us airplanes, rockets, vaccines and computers. To depart from naturalism, modernists say, is to abandon the episteme that provides technology and to retreat into a medieval mindset as the radical Islamists have done. That is why the most dogmatic modernists see little difference between non-modernist (fundamentalist) Christians and Islamists, even though their behavior is so very different.

Those who assume that the future will be a continuation of the present suppose that modernism will always retain its worldwide dominance, although localities may be temporarily taken over by Islam or some other fundamentalism. On the contrary, I predict that the foundations of modernism will be profoundly shaken in the twenty-first century as the public becomes aware that the actual data of science disconfirm the ambitious claims Darwinists make for the creative power of natural selection, and as it learns that the best metaphysical platform, even for science, lies in divine creation rather than in the fantasy that the human mind is the product of irrational forces. As the truth about creation becomes more widely known, even within the sheltered cloisters of the university, people will ask, "How could the supposedly self-correcting scientific community have been so wrong for so long about a matter of such importance?" They will also ask, "How and why was the evidence for creation suppressed and distorted for so long?" The surfacing of these questions will have a devastating effect not on *science*, understood as unbiased empirical investigation, but on the twentieth-century leadership of the scientific community, which strayed far from true science in the pursuit of fame, wealth and cultural domination.

❷ **What is the basis for tolerance, and what should be the limits of tolerance? When does an exaggerated horror of intolerance and self-righteousness become a new form of intolerance and a hatred of righteousness?**

Tolerance is one of the most systematically misunderstood topics in modernist culture. The basic error is to suppose that relativism leads to tolerance, whereas any absolute truth claim implies intolerance. There is a little superficial truth mixed with this error. If I am absolutely convinced that 2 + 2 = 4, no more and no less, then I may seem intolerant of those who want to waste my time arguing that the correct answer is 5 or 3. I am unlikely to resort to force or bribery to prove my claim, however, because it is safer and cheaper to rely on reason to convince those who will listen to reason, while allowing the obtuse or defiant to go their own way.

Disputed scientific questions are settled by experiment, a procedure ordinarily acceptable to everyone, which is why scientific controversies involve violence only under pathological circumstances, as in Stalin's Russia. When there is a high-stakes dispute involving science or philosophy or politics, and no generally acceptable way to resolve it, then contending groups may resort to browbeating, job discrimination and propaganda to ensure that their views prevail. Universities today are in disorder (outside of technical fields) mainly *because* the governing philosophy assumes an epistemological relativism. This philosophy is usually called postmodernism, but I think a better term would be *hyper-modernism,* signifying that it is essentially scientific naturalism carried to its logical conclusion. Because science deals with facts and not values, modernist universities increasingly lack a nonarbitrary basis for deciding even such basic value questions as the difference between good and evil. Were Lenin and Osama bin Laden truly evil, or were they merely acting according to standards that are different from ours but in which they sincerely believed? Ask a question like that in one of our hyper-modernist academic departments and be prepared to receive a barrage of equivocation.

The true basis for tolerance is a religious view of mankind that requires tolerance because it teaches that every kind of authority has the potential to become abusive. Any dominant religion may be more or less tolerant of other beliefs, but if it wishes to remain dominant it must decide by its own lights what to tolerate and how much tolerance it can afford to extend. For example, scientific naturalists typically will tolerate Christianity provided that Christian doctrines are confined to private life and not proposed as a basis for lawmaking or employed in public education. The Church of England of the seventeenth and eighteenth centuries seems intolerant by modern standards because it didn't fully tolerate religious minorities, but by the standards of the time, simply to permit religious dissidents to practice their faith in private was admirably tolerant. As long as the Roman Catholic Church seemingly still aspired to govern and not merely to be tolerated within a culture dominated by Protestantism, Protestants were understandably wary of Catholic ambitions. The dominant creed may aspire to be tolerant, but to remain dominant it must decide by its own criteria what the proper limits of tolerance should be. If there are no limits to tolerance, then there is no basis for fighting even murder or oppression. Why not allow a Hitler or Stalin to do as he likes in "his" territory as long as he grants us a liberty to oppress whomever we like in "our" territory?

Domestically, should we allow some favored groups to preach or practice racial or religious intolerance while requiring others to obey a very different standard?

An exaggerated or selective enforcement of tolerance, or "sensitivity," can easily become a pretext for new forms of oppression. The prime oppressive ideology in current America is termed "political correctness," the foundation of which is the view that the greatest sins are intolerance and insensitivity. Philosophically, political correctness has links to Marxism, but I prefer to give it the more generic label of "victimism." The basic premise of victimism is that society is divided into two categories of persons, victims and oppressors. The oppressors are always wrong, and the victims are always right. The goal of political activity (and everything is deemed to be political) is to disempower the oppressors and to empower the victims, often so that they can do some oppressing of their own. Anyone who has spent much time in one of our great universities will know what I mean. Rules that were formerly thought to be absolute, such as freedom of thought and expression, are discarded whenever the victims' interests so demand. An oppressor who says something that offends a designated victim is sentenced to sensitivity training, but the victims may abuse the oppressors all they like.

Victimism is supposedly based on a passion for tolerance, but the passion lasts only until the victims have enough power to turn on the oppressors. Under the rules of victimism, tolerating the oppressors is absurd. Of course, this philosophy is self-contradictory. If the victims truly were victims, they would not be given the extraordinary advantages that victim status confers. The designated "victims" really are victimized in another sense, however; because often the effect of the philosophy is to keep the victims in a state of dependency so they can be manipulated by demagogues.

People who are festering with resentment for real and imagined grievances can be persuaded that their welfare depends on following bullies and extortionists who promise to wrest concessions from the oppressors. One of the right questions is, "How can we help the victims to understand that the manipulators who endeavor to keep them in a state of sullen resentment are their worst enemies?"

❸ When we do have to fight oppression or aggression, what methods should we employ, and what limits should we respect?

For warfare to be just, the means must be proportionate to the end, and unnecessary killing or cruelty must be avoided. However, a broader principle is required than simply the avoidance of unnecessary cruelty. This principle is applicable not only to actual warfare but also to cultural conflicts that may be loosely called "wars" but are waged solely with words and arguments. In the simplest language, in all cases it is as important to win the peace as it is to win the war.

We can see this illustrated in the problems faced by the United States as it prepared to act against the Islamist terrorists and the nations that sponsored or protected them. America had the raw military power to obliterate all these nations with nuclear bombs. Of course, that would have been immoral, and it would also have resulted in a more dangerous situation than that which had called forth the use of force. The United States would hardly be the gainer if it defeated Afghanistan and then found itself faced with the enduring hatred of a billion or more Muslims, as well as a badly divided population at home.

The question here is not whether military force should ever be used. I do not doubt the necessity of taking forcible action to overthrow the oppressive Taliban government in Afghanistan. The problem is how to use force so that it results not just in a military victory (difficult enough to achieve in itself) but in a much healthier political situation, rather than an embittered Afghani population and a steadily increasing terrorist problem, however that may be defined.

Avoiding the use of excessive force is not the only application of the principle. It is also important not to stop with half-measures, which kill people and enrage the enemy without achieving the objectives for which the battle was joined. That is what the United States did in Vietnam. Because President Lyndon Johnson could not decide between his domestic objectives and his international security objectives, he failed to achieve either one. The American military achieved a spectacular victory in the Gulf War, but the United States lost the peace because the first President Bush decided to leave the tyrant Saddam Hussein in power. Using either too much force to win the peace or too little force to win the war may produce a disaster.

The application of my two-sided principle extends beyond conflict between nations. In previous writing I have described my own campaign against the oppressive intellectual domination of our culture by Darwinian materialism. This domination has extended even to Christian colleges where professors are fearful of displeasing their secular intellectual overlords. On occasion someone will suggest to me that the way to deal with this situation is to bring pressure to bear against the Christian colleges to fire professors who are not teaching correct biblical principles. I see this as an example of a cure that would be worse than the disease. Threats of firings would merely unify the erring professors in defense of each other and allow them to justify their timidity on the basis of academic freedom. What is intolerable about the situation is not that some professors hold incorrect views but that they use their authority to exclude better views from the campus environments, thus curtailing the self-corrective processes of free debate and discussion. The way to cure this situation is to open up the Christian colleges to genuine intellectual freedom rather than to shut freedom of discussion down even further.

I titled one of my books *Defeating Darwinism by Opening Minds*, and I have told many lecture audiences that opening minds is the *only* appropriate way to defeat Darwinism. An oppressive philosophy should be defeated only by removing the oppression, not by substituting a contrary form of oppression. I insisted that we in the Wedge would defeat Darwinism by opening minds or we would not defeat it at all. On the other hand, I was also deaf to the many entreaties I received to be content with half-measures by accepting important elements of Darwinism if they were prettified by a veneer of piety. I had to strike deeply enough to reach the crucial error and also to employ only tactics that rest on the principles which the better elements in academic life will always regard as essential to the practice of truth-seeking. The means of conflict must be chosen and employed so as to win both the war and the peace.

SIX

Genesis and Gender

The Transgendered Son: Guess Who's Coming to Dinner?

Near the end of the twentieth century I read a brief story about family life by a professor at one of our most self-consciously politically correct universities. The professor and his wife described themselves as feminists against homophobia, and they were not hypocrites. They were very willing to apply their philosophy to their personal and family lives. Had their son told them he was homosexual, for example, they would have concealed any private misgivings and shouted the required approval. But the son told them instead that he was "transgendered," and their readings in the gender-bending literature of feminism and queer theory had not prepared them to understand that a still more radical challenge to traditional sex roles might appear in their own home. The resulting dialogue read like a parody of what many parents have endured, desperately trying to understand why their offspring insist on doing embarrassing things like coloring their hair incandescent, getting tattooed or putting rings through their noses and studs in their tongues. They asked, "So what does this mean?"

The son answered, "It means I'm a girl. I want to wear dresses and makeup and challenge the whole patriarchal, bourgeois idea of gender."

This announcement sent the parents close to panic because they were expecting distinguished dinner guests that very night. I do not mean that they had invited some paragon of stuffy respectability like a parson or a judge, or even unenlightened relatives who were still under the impression that boys are boys and girls are girls. No, that very night they were hosting two of the most famous public intellectuals of 1990s postmodernism, and what they feared was that even Mr. and Mrs. Stanley Fish might think their son was making a fool of himself and his parents. The father described what he feared: "I imagined my son swirling down the stairs, arriving at dinner like Loretta Young in flowing chiffon. How exactly would I explain such a phenomenon to my guests over hors d'oeuvres?" Fortunately the son dressed neutrally and stuck to relatively safe topics like religion and politics.

After the distinguished guests had departed, the embarrassing son told his parents that he had picked up the concept of transgendering from the same authors that the father assigned to his college students, trendy literary theorists like Michel Foucault and Judith Butler. If the son was pushing the envelope, he was doing so on the basis of assumptions that commanded at least a semantic consensus in the fin-de-siècle culture, a consensus implicit in the ubiquitous substitution of the term *gender* for *sex*.

Sex is a biological fact, but gender is the sort of thing French nouns have, an arbitrary designation that may just as easily be otherwise. There are only two sexes, but there can be as many genders as human imagination cares to invent, and one can in principle switch back and forth between them at will. Start from that ideological base, which the parents never questioned, and the son was merely putting into practice the implicit invitation to choose (or invent) his own gender. He was not rebelling against the family philosophy but trying to live by it.

Pinned by his own logic, the dismayed father reacted like a 1940s liberal who has just been told that a Negro family is buying the house next door. "I suddenly felt rage toward those ivory-towered theoreticians who glibly spout gender theories," raged the father, who very nearly fit into that category himself. Shouldn't they have foreseen the humiliation it would cause a decent father like himself to see his son wearing a dress? Perhaps the boy could be shamed out of that dress and accompanying underwear.

But he couldn't, and instead he expressed his disgust at the hypocrisy of parents who lacked the courage of their own convictions. The transgendered son felt entitled not just to tolerance but to approval, and so he began insisting that the parents start referring to him as "s/he" and as their daughter. The parents received no support for their half-hearted resistance from friends, neighbors or relatives, who all told them such experimentation was common these days and they shouldn't be so inflexible about it. Eventually they had to make the best of the situation, and soon the father was even using his son/daughter as a positive example in his classes. "After all," he rationalized, "I wasn't losing a son but gaining a daughter." Another interpretation would be that he was gaining a very mixed-up exhibitionist pretending to be a daughter.

Pinned by Our Own Logic

It would be easy to take cheap shots at the parents. I can resist the temptation because I too have been a parent pinned by his own logic, and I also know how easy it is to pick up very foolish notions when everyone around you accepts them as the latest in avant-garde wisdom. My reaction to the story was not to ridicule but to pity, and to reflect on how both the father's confusion and the son's preposterous rebellion grew logically from ideas that are so taken for granted in the academic world that it would be difficult to find a professor who could forcefully and persuasively refute them. Our sons and daughters take off from the platform we give them, and by the time we realize how skewed we have allowed that platform to become, it is too late to start over. Something similar happens to teachers, because ideas have consequences. We tell students that they can be authentic persons only if they choose their own values, tacitly assuming that they will choose values that we can approve or at least tolerate. What if they don't? The story of the transgendered son is similar to that of the American Taliban soldier in the preceding chapter, except that it mercifully ended merely in absurdity rather than in crime.

The two stories typify for me the fractured state of hyper-modernist culture, particularly in its educational institutions, from public schools to our finest universities. The scientific and technological faculties know pretty much what they want to teach, are successful in educating their students in the traditions and practices of their science, and are not inclined to take seriously any outsiders who say that there is something inadequate about their way of thinking. The biological sciences in particular are currently rulers of the academic roost, with ample funding generated by their (mainly unfulfilled) promises of prodigious advances in the conquest of disease. Contemporary biologists invoke their authority to ridicule any suggestion that organisms are designed by a purposeful intelligence, and they also scorn any remnant of teleology, the idea that organisms, including humans, exist for some purpose other than merely to survive and reproduce. The resulting philosophical indoctrination has a lot to do with why students pick up such confused ideas about sexuality. For example, Darwinists insist that birds do not fly because they were *meant* to fly but because they happened to evolve that potential and then exploited it in order to survive and reproduce.

For the same reasons, the teachers all assume that humans do not reproduce sexually in order to further some purpose of a Creator. Students learn that sexual reproduction evolved by accident and then spread from one species to another because it provided some advantage to the species that happened to reproduce that way. Once we understand that life has no ultimate purpose, we are free to divorce sex from reproduction and employ it entirely for sensual pleasure or personal assertion. The fact of sex may have its origins in biology, but Darwinian biology has no normative implications for how we should live today. Darwinism enabled humans to declare their independence from the primal biblical teaching on sexuality: Genesis 1:27.

So God created humankind in his image,
  in the image of God he created them;
male and female he created them.

Today the substitution of the term *gender* for *sex* signifies our declaration of independence from biology as well. Begin with Genesis, and you are on a logical track that leads to the conclusion that our sexuality reflects God's purpose for our lives. Begin instead with Darwinism, and fantastic as the suggestion would have seemed to Darwin or Huxley, you are on a logical track that leads ultimately to the transgendered son. Think of it this way: if it was wrong for the son to conclude that his male "gender" was something arbitrarily imposed on him by culture, then where did his logic go wrong? I believe it went wrong at a very early stage. His education in a confused culture concealed from him a fundamental fact about human beings and their sexuality which he needed to know. The point of life is not to have your own way about everything but to become the person God meant you to be. An education that started with Genesis would have taught him about that fact and its significance.

In modern culture the technocrats know pretty well what they want to accomplish and how to educate the young to further their program. In contrast, the literary professors are uncertain of what society expects of them. On the whole they are poorly funded, and they would have difficulty stating a defensible educational mission that could justify even the limited funding that they have. The most obvious role for the humanities would be to supply the knowledge of life's value and purpose that science by definition excludes from its own territory. Indeed, that was the original role for humanities courses when the universities stopped teaching theology and needed a substitute. Many literary professors still want to play that role, but how are they to do it? The need is real, for the success of technology requires some counterbalance, some way of gaining knowledge about the ends to which technology should be put. What gets in the way of that project is the cultural definition of *knowledge,* which allows only for a knowledge of means and not of ultimate ends, and excludes concepts essential to any understanding of value and purpose.

For example, the notion that there is an objectively knowable right and wrong which a person can elect to follow is profoundly unscientific. Science knows nothing of free, rational agents whose choices are uncaused, nor of a moral realm that is not of human invention. A strictly scientific (materialist) epistemology implies that ethical theory is founded on illusions. (For details, see chapter five of *The Wedge of Truth.*) Illusions may be preserved for a while if they seem useful, but they blow away like smoke when they are seriously challenged by people bearing the authority to define reality. Long ago educational institutions would have delegated the values curriculum to a Bible or theology faculty, which could refer to its own real entities outside of science. In those days science was a relatively minor part of the curriculum precisely because it was thought to be incapable of dealing with the most important subjects. During the twentieth century, however, nearly all institutions of higher education abandoned any theological basis for moral knowledge as a lost cause because of the perceived implications of advancing scientific knowledge.

The triumph of Darwinism established that we could not look

to a Creator for moral guidance, although men might invoke a
theological tradition to give some religious blessing to moral ideas
actually derived from a secular source. The Creator came to be
seen as a sort of imaginary policeman in the sky (see chapter one
of *The Wedge of Truth*), who retained a certain utility in enforcing
morality among the unenlightened but who could no longer be
taken seriously by the educated classes as a source of knowledge.
What could fill the Creator's place as the ultimate source of moral
teaching? The answer was (in various formulations) something
like the "Western heritage" that President Clinton invoked, as
described in chapter one of this book, when he referred to "our
oldest and most cherished human values."

In universities this premise typically took the concrete form of
a survey course in Western civilization, which identified the foundation of cultural values with a literary tradition rather than a
divine revelation. In its original formulation this approach was an
indirect way of preserving the theological foundation, because the
giants of the Western literary tradition (such as Dante, Chaucer,
Shakespeare, Milton) drew their moral inspiration from biblical
authority. Only after skeptics had time to sight their artillery on
the new target did it become apparent that the castle of literary values was built on a foundation of sand. If we find values in literature, then where does literature find them?

If literature finds these values only in an ungrounded tradition,
then we are probably relying on a tribal prejudice rather than on
truths of universal applicability. Perhaps our oldest and most cherished values are steeped in evils like racism, sexism, homophobia
and speciesism. Such suspicion inspired the derision of the cam-

pus mobs who dismissed the literary canon as a bunch of "dead white males" and who chanted "Ho! Ho! Heave ho! Western Civ has got to go!" Like the transgendered son, they were not rebelling against what they had been taught but taking the logic of their teachers one step further. In the course of time the chanting protesters became professors themselves, and they propounded nihilistic theories based on what they had learned in college.

If literary studies deal primarily with values, and if science teaches us that there can be knowledge only of facts and not of values, then literary studies must logically become another kind of technology, the technology of using words to achieve goals generated by subjective desire. This is the genesis of what hyper-modern literary professors call "theory," the use of literary analysis for political or ideological purposes. Semantic manipulation really is a powerful tool for shaping public opinion. Whatever we think of this definition of the literary enterprise, we must acknowledge that in some respects it has been successful. The power to alter the language of life in the genome may be awesome, but the power to alter the terms that editorial and textbook writers employ is scarcely less awesome. Persuading the writers to use ideologically loaded terms like *homophobia* and *gender* as if they were purely descriptive prepared the cognitive territory for a brave new moral landscape into which the transgendered son advanced recklessly, like an unequipped novice mountaineer starting up the Matterhorn alone.

The last two decades of the twentieth century have produced an avalanche of academic writing on gender, along with research centers and courses focusing on the correlated issues of feminism and homosexuality. The textbooks for such courses start with the assumption that *gender* refers to the social roles attached to biological sex. In this view femininity and masculinity are mere social constructs. *Sex* refers to biology, whereas *gender* describes the way one is socialized according to some standard of behavior associated with a sex. Only women can bear children, but in hyper-modernist culture, women are not the only ones who can be mothers or daughters.

What About Genesis?

The story of the transgendered son reminded me of the book of Genesis and of its continuing importance. In my role as the leading edge of the Wedge of Truth, attempting to make the initial penetration into the intellectual monopoly of scientific naturalism, I needed to stay away from the book of Genesis. I did not want to become involved in the long-standing and deadlocked battle between the Bible and science. Rather I wanted to point out that the real battle is not between the Bible and science but between science as unbiased, empirical observation on the one hand, and science as applied naturalistic philosophy on the other. To put that issue clearly before the public, I moved away from the creation account in Genesis as the primary Scripture and urged people to begin instead with the most important teaching about the meaning of creation in the Bible, the prologue to the Gospel of John. In chapter two of this book I explained how I contrasted the first words of John—"In the beginning was the Word"—with the first words of the scientific materialist creation story: "In the beginning were the particles."

I put Genesis aside temporarily so that my readers could focus their attention on the irreconcilable conflict between Darwinism and even the broadest view of divine creation. To start with Genesis tended to direct attention on the age of the earth rather than on the Darwinian mechanism. Starting with Genesis also tended to give people the impression that only the first chapters of the Bible were threatened, so that they could reconcile the Bible with evolutionary science if they were only willing to read Genesis figuratively and allow the "days" of creation to be geological periods of indefinite length rather than twenty-four-hour days. This superficial compromise tended to lead to the disastrous accommodation known as theistic evolution, where a veneer of biblical and Christian interpretation was added to camouflage a fundamentally naturalistic creation story. "In the beginning were the particles" does not negate merely the Genesis account; it negates the entire Bible from the first word to the last. It implies that while God may "exist," he does not create or do anything to "interfere" with the natural processes of the earth, at least after the ultimate beginning—perhaps the big bang. Naturalistic assumptions imply that God is, in a word, unimportant.

Placing Genesis to one side was necessary in order to bring out the true conflict between Darwinian evolution and Christian theism, and to show that the conflict could not be reconciled by the adjustment of a few words in Genesis. Using the Gospel of John instead of Genesis was successful in defining the fundamental conflict, and thus it enabled me to present the stark conflict between naturalism and Christian theism in a realistic light. Unfortunately, however, this way of arguing the issue gave some people the impression that I was permanently discarding Genesis by treating it as allegorical or at least as having no value as history. If I were actually doing that, Bible believers would have had good reason to protest. Genesis is not merely an optional add-on to the Bible; it is an essential part of the whole. The right question is not whether we are to read Genesis literally, but whether we are to read it as it was meant to be read and as Jesus, the very Word referred to in John 1, appears to have read it. If Genesis is discarded as altogether mythical, then a great deal that is essential to Christianity is at risk. As many persons have pointed out, the book of Romans makes clear the necessity of having the first Adam before the second Adam, whose sacrifice saved mankind from the consequences of the disobedience of the first Adam. In short, the question of the historical value of Genesis is important to the entire structure of the Christian gospel and must at some point be addressed.

Before getting to the main point of this chapter, which is how to frame the right questions about the reliability of Genesis as history, I need to say something about the enduring relevance of Genesis as an explanation of the most basic elements of the human condition today, as well as long ago. There are many moral teachings in Genesis. For example, in chapter four I used the story of Joseph and his brothers to illustrate how what seemed to be a pointless detour in life may, in the reality known to God, be the main road home. There are two moral teachings in particular which I believe are at the heart of the first chapters of Genesis. First, there is the story of rebellion. To try to build a perfect society or utopia for humans as we are today, after sin has entered the world, is pointless. The plan cannot succeed, and even if it could, the success would not last. If man does not have enough trouble given to him, he will rebel against his paradise and create trouble for himself. Adam and Eve lived in perfect conditions with the freedom to do almost anything they might want to do and with only one restriction, the only "no" in a paradise that was in every other respect theirs to enjoy as they pleased. Of course, the one thing that they were forbidden to do was the very thing they could not resist doing.

This disobedience is not merely a single historical event. It illustrates a permanent feature of the human condition, a feature also illustrated by the story of the transgendered son. The son lived in comfort and could do virtually whatever he wanted to do. He lived in a community where sexual experimentation and promiscuity were common, and his parents and neighbors would approve if he had whatever sexual relations he wanted, including relations with another male. There was almost nothing he could have done sexually that would have shocked his parents. So he managed to find the one thing that went beyond what even these most permissive of parents had been prepared to approve. Having found that further step in the logic, he insisted that his parents not only allow him to do it but also give him their approval. It was not enough to be tolerated; he must even be praised for his rebellion.

Here we see the rebellious human ego at work. If immature persons have something tangible to rebel against, then their rebellion may be rational. But if they are not subject to any restriction that is truly oppressive, then they will look for something that they can imagine to be oppressive and will insist on doing whatever it is that they are rightly forbidden to do, even if the rebellion leads to their own destruction.

A second major teaching of Genesis is that the difference between the sexes is fundamental to our created selves. "Male and female he created them." The notion that the sexual difference is merely one of "gender," something that humans imagined and that can be changed whenever they like, is foreign to the Bible. Today people are rebelling against the Bible's teaching, imagining that it is up to us and not (a supposedly imaginary) God to decide what the fundamental division of humanity should be. If you think that the rebellion of the transgendered son was absurd and pointless, on what basis could you justify that position? You have arrived at a conclusion (even if only by coincidence) implied by the facts laid down in the first book of the Bible rather than by the fashionable assumptions of modernism. People in our time are so ignorant of the order of creation that they imagine that the distinctions of feminine and masculine natures are things that man invented and that man can abolish or alter. I predict that our rebellion against creation will be seen in time to be harmful and even preposterous, and then we will at last realize that the teaching of Genesis about humanity remains as realistic as it has always been.

The Right Questions About Genesis

1 Assuming we now agree that the foundation of Christian theism ("In the beginning was the Word") finds much more support even in scientific evidence than the foundational assumption of scientific naturalism or materialism ("In the beginning were the particles"), should we stop with that conclusion, or should we go

on to reconsider Old Testament passages that modernists have pervasively assumed to be mythical or just false? Might some of those passages be factual after all?

I have explained that I avoided Genesis altogether in determining the initial point of entry for the thin edge of the Wedge because starting with John 1 allowed my argument to proceed from the most basic point at issue rather than to bog it down in less fundamental subjects. Having made that argument elsewhere, I will now take the preliminary steps for granted and assume that the reader agrees with me that the evidence of science shows that "in the beginning was the Word" is as true scientifically as it is true theologically, scripturally and in every other way. I will further assume that the reader is a Christian theist who believes the entire message of John 1:1-14, including the all-important statement "The Word became flesh and dwelt among us." The very Word through whom all things were created lived on earth as a man, and this is not a statement merely of "religious belief" but of *fact*.

Once we have reached that conclusion, we must take full account of the shocking circumstance that the entire weight of scientific and academic authority for the past century and more has been placed in the service of an erroneous philosophy, the philosophy of scientific naturalism or materialism. Those whom we relied on as teachers have very seriously misled us on a matter of fundamental importance. To begin the story of creation with nothing but particles in mindless motion, governed only by chance and the impersonal laws of physics, is to pick a starting place that could never lead to the world we inhabit, with its vast wonderland of living creatures. The evidence of science properly understood is that life is the product of a preexisting, unevolved intelligence. "In the beginning was the Word." We can build confidently on that fundamental truth, and if we build on its opposite, we will go very far astray, as in fact we have done. The story of the transgendered son is just one marker of how far astray we have gone by setting off in the wrong direction. If any reader is inclined to scoff at the assumptions I am defending, let him contemplate the absurdities to which materialist assumptions have led us.

We must first understand that our human wisdom called "science" has been systematically mistaken about the fact of creation and that leaders of the scientific community have taken and are still taking energetic steps to suppress dissent and to prevent the public from learning the powerful arguments against evolutionary naturalism that have existed all along. From this understanding it is logically incumbent on us to take the next step and ask whether our highly prejudiced academic culture, following the same assumptions, may have been similarly mistaken in relegating virtually the entire book of Genesis to the category of myth. Certainly we cannot afford to disregard the possibility that there is much more truth in Genesis than we had thought. The meaning of the fact of creation is most systematically explained in John, but important aspects of that fact, such as the origin and nature of sexuality and marriage, are taught only in Genesis. The extreme confusion about sexuality illustrated in the story of the transgendered son has its roots in the rejection of the biblical doctrine of creation, a doctrine we cannot hope to understand unless we learn from both John and Genesis.

2 **If we are going to screw up enough courage to ponder whether the early chapters of Genesis have value as history rather than merely as myth or allegory, what chapter should we examine first?**

As always my ambition in this book is not to solve all the problems that the Bible poses for people like ourselves who have been educated in modernist ways of thinking, but only to be as helpful as I can be by framing the right questions in the right order, so that more highly qualified Christians will have the best possible chance of finding answers that I cannot see. Just as I said that Genesis is not the best place to start when considering the truth of the Bible as a whole, I also think that Genesis 1 is not the best place to start when considering the historical value of the account of creation in Genesis. I want to begin with some important points on which Bible-believing Christians agree, although the secular world does not agree with them, and then to move on from that basis in agreement to address any subjects about which Christians do not agree. I do not want to begin with a disagreement because that will lead nowhere.

A conversation with a friend named John alerted me to the point I am making in this section. John is a very dedicated Christian, well educated in geology, who takes the "old earth" or progressive creationist position on Genesis. John's life has been so transformed by Christ that it would be absurd to question either his sincerity or his willingness to defy modernist fashions in thought. John takes the position he does because he believes that the evidence of geology strongly supports it, and that it involves a perfectly legitimate interpretation of the word *day* as it's used in

Genesis, not a strained interpretation crafted to dodge modernist objections.

In our conversation I carelessly referred to the competing young-earth or recent creation position as the "Genesis position," and John rightly corrected me for making a question-begging assumption. John told me how strongly he had been affected when he had made a similar careless error in referring to Psalm 90 as a "psalm of David," like so many others. A pastor pointed out to him that Psalm 90 is actually attributed to Moses, and this is of particular significance because Moses is identified as the human author of Genesis—not only by Jewish and Christian traditions but by the words of Jesus himself. Anyone who disputes the Mosaic authorship of Genesis is definitely headed toward theological liberalism, and neither John or I was going that way.

You can see the advantage of starting with a point of agreement. The prayer of Moses in Psalm 90 states that

> a thousand years in your sight
> > are like yesterday when it is past,
> > or like a watch in the night. (Ps 90:4)

"From that I think that the old-earth position *is* the Genesis position," John commented. I agreed that John had made an excellent point, but I began to ponder what Moses had said a little later in the same prayer:

> The days of our life are seventy years,
> > or perhaps eighty, if we are strong. (Ps 90:10)

That reminded me that the author of Genesis had said very specifically and in detail in Genesis 5 that the early patriarchs lived phenomenally long lives by our standards, and even fathered sons after having lived for centuries. Yet Moses knew very well that the lifespan in his own time was much shorter. Some attempts have been made to interpret the lifespans of Genesis 5 figuratively, but the attempts have always struck me as very lame. I can see no reason why Moses would have given such very specific figures unless he believed that they were true, and I am at a loss to understand why Moses believed them to be true and why so many people then and for centuries to come accepted them as factual, unless they had substantial reason to believe that the figures *were* true. Ancient peoples did not have to wait for modern science to determine the normal human lifespan; they knew it very well from observation, and yet they were confident that some people had once lived much longer.

Interpreting the lifespans in Genesis 5 is not a problem for modernists, who readily assume that they know more about ancient times than the ancients did, and who can always apply modernist tools of biblical criticism—essentially, evolutionary naturalism applied to the Bible—to explain away any mysteries. It is a problem for those of us who reject evolutionary naturalism as a philosophy, both when it is imposed on biology and when it is imposed on the Bible. Assuming that Moses really was the author of Genesis, I propose that we consider seriously that he knew something we do not.

The world has been taught to assume that the long lifespans specified in Genesis 5 are absurd, and if we agree with the world, we will hardly save the credibility of the author of Genesis by reinterpreting a few words. But suppose we are willing to brave the world's ridicule to insist that we be allowed to take seriously the possibility that the named early patriarchs really did live as long as Genesis 5 says they did. If we proceed from that premise, then a great deal of very interesting speculation and theorizing must follow. For example, how different must the physical conditions have been in those ancient times to permit people to have lived for so long? When and why did the conditions change so much that the human lifespan was greatly reduced? I would have hesitated to propose such daring questions for investigation until very recently, but I am encouraged to do so now by what I have learned about the blindness of modernist prejudices through my study of Darwinism and of the consistent unwillingness of Darwinists to consider evidence or reasoning that supports conclusions that they do not welcome. Some of what we have been indoctrinated to accept as unchallengeable fact turns out to be deduced from naturalistic philosophy and never rigorously tested by experiment, in particular, the claim that natural selection of random genetic variants has the fantastic creative power to account for the complex wonders of plants and animals. Viewed scientifically and without prejudice, the claims of Darwinism are more fantastic than anything stated in Genesis 5. With the fall of Darwinism now in prospect, it is time to invite unprejudiced scientific investigation into the possibility that human beings thousands of years ago may have had longer life spans than they do now, or than they did at the time Psalm 90 was composed.

❸ Could a scientific research project into the lifespans of Genesis 5 be productively pursued?

All that is necessary to research the lifespans in Genesis 5 is to put aside the philosophical dogma of uniformitarianism and proceed instead on the assumption that the basic "constants" of physics may have changed over time. Performing research on this philosophically liberated basis may suggest answers to a variety of puzzles, and even allow us to return on a more scientifically informed basis to the question of how to interpret the time scale of creation. I am not opposed to discussing the days of Genesis 1 or any other topic, but I think most of us will be better prepared to do so after we have had the opportunity to think through the full implications of what we conclude about Genesis 5.

When I raise questions of this sort with scientists, their usual response is to dismiss the irritating questions with ridicule or to deny that there is any proof that changes in the physical constants have occurred. This is a classic example of getting the answer ahead of the question. There rarely is proof of anything interesting until people have a reason to look for it. The right place to begin a research program is with a hypothesis. What changes would need to have occurred to make it possible for the early patriarchs to live as long as Genesis 5 says they did? If theory suggests that there is a hypothetical set of constants that *would* permit very long lives if it had once existed, then there will be a sufficient motive to look for evidence that the constants actually *have* changed over time.

I make no dogmatic claims. I predict that scientists who are genuinely trying to find a set of physical conditions that would permit greatly extended human lifespans will be able to do so in good faith, but the accuracy of any prediction can be determined only in the light of what actually transpires. Once the right questions are asked, further inquiry may point to a way of supporting the lifespans of Genesis 5, or it may not. All I can say before the effort is made is that we will never know the answer unless we ask the right questions, and so we must not allow ourselves to be intimidated from doing so by the predictable materialist rant and ridicule. Once we have defied that bluff with respect to Darwinism itself, we should be liberated to seek the truth wherever it can be found.

SEVEN

Truth and Liberty

FREEDOM TO DISSENT
AND FREEDOM TO DO RIGHT

John Stuart Mill and the Freedom to Dissent

In his renowned Victorian-era essay *On Liberty*, John Stuart Mill began his argument by observing that the benefits of constitutional democracy in government are not adequate to protect individuals from the coercive power that can be exercised by a majority. Even where the majority chooses not to enforce its will with formal legal restraints and penalties, nonconforming individuals may be intimidated by what Mill called "the tyranny of the prevailing opinion and feeling," which exerts informal but still powerful limits on what individuals may say or do without suffering some penalty such as social ostracism or denial of career advancement.

Mill used the example of religious opinion, about which in his day formal legal restraints had generally been abolished, though constraints of custom remained. A man who voiced unpopular religious opinions would not be jailed, but his prospects for advancement in society would suffer. "So natural to mankind is intolerance in whatever they really care about," Mill wrote, "that religious freedom has hardly anywhere been practicably realized except where religious indifference, which dislikes to have its peace disturbed by theological quarrels, has added its weight to the scale." Although Mill did not make the point, his logic would lead one to expect that the religiously indifferent would be as intolerant in their way as the religiously committed, but the object of their intolerance would be those religious opinions that threaten to disturb the peace of society by raising matters of theological controversy. If the religiously indifferent were to become the dominant party in society, then the expression of *any* ardent religious opinion might become the sort of social transgression that ensures that one will never again be invited to fashionable dinner parties or considered suitable to hold a responsible position requiring good judgment.

To see how this might work, try this thought experiment. Suppose you were being considered for a junior professorship at Yale, an editorial position at a newspaper or television news department, or a job as a lawyer at a blue-chip law firm. At a social occasion during the job recruitment process, would you feel free to disclose that you attend a charismatic church or vote for political candidates whom the media have described as belonging to the "religious right"? No one denies that you have every legal right to do these things, but you had better keep quiet about it, or you may learn the hard way about the tyranny of the prevailing opinion and feeling. The prevailing opinion may change from time to time, and may be different in San Francisco from what it is in Peoria, but there will always be a prevailing opinion, and to defy it will always be costly to those who want to get along in the world. It is therefore a little amusing that the eminent philosopher John Stuart Mill gained enduring fame by proposing a platitudinous remedy for the universal disease of social intolerance, as if a medical writer were to suggest chicken soup or aspirin for all the ailments of the body.

Mill wrote (slightly paraphrased) that his object was to assert one very simple principle: the only purpose for which power can be rightfully exercised over any member of a civilized community against his will is to prevent him from harming others. He cannot be compelled to do anything or to refrain from doing anything because it will make him happier or because, in the opinion of others, to do so would be wise, or even right. These are good reasons for remonstrating with him or reasoning with him or persuading or entreating him, but not for compelling him or causing him any sort of harm if he does otherwise. To justify that, the conduct from which it is desired to deter him must be thought to produce harm to someone else. "The only part of the conduct of any one, for which he is amenable to society, is that which concerns others. In the part which merely concerns himself, his independence is . . . absolute. Over himself, over his own body and mind, the individual is sovereign."

It's not so simple. As a recent former president might have said, it all depends on what you mean by *harm* and also on whether there is really any part of a person's conduct which "merely concerns himself," although it sufficiently bothers others that they want to go to the trouble of all that remonstrating, reasoning, entreating and, finally, compelling. Mill's "very simple principle" is in fact open-ended to the point of being nearly meaningless and invites endless disputation about how it might apply, for example, to adulterers, alcoholics, smokers, film stars who glamorize smoking, purveyors and readers of pornography, and especially to parents or persons who may one day have parental responsibilities, which is to say most people.

A great poet wrote that "no man is an island," and certainly that is particularly true of any person who has responsibilities to others which he may not be able to fulfill if he does not take care of his body, his mind and his property. In a democracy we all participate in government, so we are to a degree concerned with each other's mental and physical health. Since irresponsible parenting causes a host of evils, society has at least some interest in discouraging conduct or opinions that may encourage irresponsibility in any of its members. For example, if it becomes respectable to think of marriage as a mere civil contract rather than as a sacred bond that is unbreakable except under extraordinary circumstances, then the incidence of divorce will surely increase, with consequences for society that have become evident in our time.

Vague as it is, Mill's principle appeals to the liberal imagination, and Mill himself is sometimes called the saint of liberalism. We could say that *On Liberty* was the founding document of twentieth-century liberalism—and of its moral degeneracy, if you disapprove of the lengths to which Mill's principle has been taken—just as Darwin's *Origin of Species* was the founding document of evolutionary naturalism.

I encountered John Stuart Mill and Sigmund Freud at about the same time, as a college student. Together they encouraged a way of thinking that seems to come naturally to immature young adults, who want to do whatever is pleasurable and fashionable, and who wish to have a rationalization that is powerful enough not only to justify their own conduct but also to shame those who do not do likewise. We students were encouraged in the idea that the admirable person was one who had the temerity to reject the "repressive" morality that we had learned in childhood and that was feebly enforced by the waning moral coercion of public opinion. If we did what our bodies wanted to do, we were sure that we would not be hurting anybody else, sin having been discarded as an obsolete and ridiculous concept.

We thought it followed that adults were tyrannical and hypocritical if they disapproved of what we were doing, and the adults eventually bowed to this moral coercion and stopped disapproving. The sexual revolution of the 1970s was immensely encouraged by this logic. I went to college before the sexual revolution, but the ideas that led to it were already becoming part of that coercive prevailing opinion. One of Mill's unintended legacies is that those who wish to impose an authoritarian control on the opinions of others give themselves ideological cover by claiming to be skeptics or bold dissenters. The "skeptics" are typically skeptical only about the orthodoxies of yesteryear or the opinions of their adversaries, while they are blindly credulous with respect to the ruling orthodoxy of our own time. A 1990s network television show titled *Politically Incorrect* symbolized this widespread practice of psuedo-dissent. The show was consistently politically correct, and of course it would not have attracted much advertising revenue for the network if it were not.

The radical aspect of Mill's principle was not merely that self-regarding conduct should be free from legal penalties but that conduct which deserved to be free from legal penalties should also be free from the coercive impact of public disapproval. This radical version of liberal individualism took about a century to become established. For example, divorce still carried a social stigma well into the twentieth century, long after the legal restrictions on divorce had been greatly relaxed. Married persons who were determined to divorce could find a way to do it, but not without incurring substantial social penalties. A divorced woman would not be received in polite society, and a divorced man might find his career blocked due to the widespread view that a man who could not manage his family life should not be trusted to manage a company.

All that has changed enormously. In my own childhood we were taught to pity the only boy in school whose parents were divorced. What chance did he have to grow up as a young man should? Now I have heard college students speak with bemusement of unusual friends who have "married parents," meaning biological parents who are still married to each other. In some countries marriage itself has largely been abandoned. People just cohabit, hetero- or homosexually as they prefer, changing their arrangements as it becomes convenient to do so. The guiding assumption seems to be that all this exercise of sexual freedom is self-regarding behavior that does not "harm others."

The consequences for children are profound, even if we assume that the adults in question do their best to care for any children who happen to be involved, within the context of their own liberated relationships. Heather may have two mommies, and Bobby may have a mother and her boyfriend, but the assorted parents all try to be kind to Heather and Bobby, at least as long as they choose to stay together in the quasi-family relationship. If they choose instead to alter their living arrangements, it will not be difficult to find a rationalization in the form of a study claiming that children are quite resilient in overcoming whatever harmful effects accompany such disruptions. Sexual experimentation even for parents is widely considered to be not only permissible but praiseworthy, whereas remaining in a relationship that is no longer fulfilling may be taken to signify a lack of personal integrity.

Mill qualified his absolute principle with the proviso that he meant it to apply "only to human beings in the maturity of their faculties," and not to youths below whatever age the law might fix as the beginning of adulthood. "Those who are still in a state to require being taken care of by others," he wrote, "must be protected against their own actions as well as against external injury." What Mill did not explain was how society would be able to persuade young persons that it was wrongful for them to engage in forbidden pleasurable activities when society approves those same activities for adults. Once public opinion endorses the view that sex outside of marriage is a permissible pleasure and that undesired consequences should be prevented by condoms and abortions rather than by abstinence, then hot-blooded adolescents are likely to consider it unfair that they should be denied pleasures so widely enjoyed by adults. Adults may say that what is good for them is bad for teenagers, but why should the teenagers believe them? Engaging in the forbidden behavior, whether sex or smoking, predictably became attractive as a badge of adulthood. Retaining moral standards for young people which adults have abandoned for themselves is not easy. Nor is it surprising that, as teenagers become on the average more immature but eager to enjoy adult pleasures, they will lobby with some success for a lowering of the age of adulthood.

Some ominous implications arise from the concept that self-regarding nonconformists have a vaguely defined right to be free not only from legal penalties but even from the moral coercion of public opinion. Does this mean that the conforming majority has no right to disapprove or to express its disapproval in gossip, unfavorable letters of recommendation or public statements? If Mill is in a sense the father of twentieth-century liberal individualism, he seems also to have fathered the notion that some individuals have a right to be protected from the disapproval of others. That notion underlies such hyper-modern practices as sensitivity training, to which individuals who offend the protected people by some word or facial expression may be sentenced for thought reform. Of course that is not what Mill had in mind, but ideas once out in the world may take on a life of their own.

In short, Mill proclaimed a very vaguely defined right and proposed that it be given potentially expansive protection even from disapproval. He built this tower of protection on a very slender philosophical base. Mill was raised by his father to be a utilitarian who judged every act or rule by its consequences, meaning its tendency to decrease the amount of pain in the world or increase the amount of pleasure. This is another "very simple principle," and Mill never departed altogether from the family philosophy, even when it would have helped his argument greatly to do so. Hence he made no appeal to religious doctrine or universal human rights. He wrote on the contrary that "I forego any advantage which could be derived to my argument from the idea of abstract right, as a thing independent of utility. I regard utility as the ultimate appeal on all ethical questions, but it must be utility in the largest sense, grounded on the permanent interests of man as a progressive being." That leaves both the liberty of one individual to do as he likes and the liberty of others to express their disapproval at the mercy of the dominant understanding of the permanent interests of man as a progressive being. Utilitarianism is a notoriously radical doctrine that upsets every settled moral rule. Dostoyevsky's student Raskolnikov used it to rationalize a robbery/murder, and utilitarian philosophers in our time have endorsed infanticide, involuntary euthanasia and sex with animals. It is hardly surprising that a liberty based only on utility should become a vehicle for new forms of repression when applied in a society that is very different from the Victorian England that Mill knew.

I will illustrate some of the contemporary consequences that Mill's ideas have had—when interpreted by minds less generous than his own—with examples from the corner of the world I know best, the greatest American universities.

In theory principles of constitutional law and academic freedom guarantee to professors, and even to students, the right to say just about anything they like, short of inciting a riot, about almost any subject, including religion, politics or science. This is formally correct up to a point in that for many years it was unusual for university authorities even to attempt disciplinary action against a professor for expression of opinions, including opinions that were obnoxious to the authorities and to other professors. In recent years, however, new concepts such as "hate speech" and "insensitivity" have circumscribed even the formal protection of freedom of expression. If I were asked whether universities now protect freedom of expression regarding religion, politics or sexual preferences, I would answer something like this: Freedom to advocate agnosticism or to oppose Christianity is zealously protected, and instructors sometimes exercise this freedom in the classroom in coercive ways, by ridiculing students who hold conservative religious views and encouraging other students to join in the ridicule.

Freedom to advocate Christian theism or oppose agnosticism is not entirely absent, but its protection is much more tenuous. A teacher who took a strong stand in favor of Christian theism would undoubtedly be accused of violating the constitutional doctrine of separation of church and state. A teacher who took an equally strong stand in favor of atheism, or even of Islam, would run no comparable risk. Freedom to advocate that homosexuality is at least as morally worthy as heterosexuality is secure, but freedom to oppose this proposition is nearly absent. Freedom to advocate what are loosely called "liberal" (leftist) political programs is secure. Freedom to oppose those programs is formally protected, but a professor who relies on that freedom had better be careful to employ only tactful language.

I recall an audience of feminist law students glaring at me fiercely because I had raised some cautious doubts about the morality of an unrestricted right to abortion. I was a senior professor who had been specifically invited to address that topic, so I had nothing to fear. The incident did serve to remind me, however, why it is often difficult for organizers of that kind of forum to find a professor who is willing to take a position that the legal or university community very passionately dislikes. The new orthodoxy we call political correctness has an effect even in formal disciplinary proceedings, but I will say no more about that because the explicit regulations are much less important than the informal tyranny of the prevailing opinion and feeling. What professors fear is not that they will be formally charged in disciplinary proceedings but that they will receive unfavorable teaching evaluations from students and unfavorable peer reviews from colleagues. Formal rules of academic freedom do not help the professor who is denied a promotion because students don't like his teaching, or who loses all his research funding because his peers do not like his ideas.

Readers of the critique to this point may suppose that I see nothing good in Mill's writing, but that is far from accurate. It is true that Mill did not present anything resembling a coherent system, and he hardly could have done that from his starting point in utilitarianism. Some of his ideas have even had a pernicious effect, which I am sure he did not intend but which perhaps he should have foreseen. That said, *On Liberty* contains marvelous passages to which I wish persons in authority would pay more attention. Even Mill's slavish devotion to utility led him to some wonderful insights that would greatly increase intellectual freedom if the most influential teachers and authors of today were to take them to heart.

Mill was at his best when he defended a very broadly defined right to dissent from the prevailing opinion on any subject, and defended it not merely because it is in the interest of the dissenter to possess such a right but particularly because it is in the interest of society to subject even its most cherished doctrines to a forceful critique from dissenters. Mill argued that the governing majority should never attempt to prevent a dissenting opinion from having a fair hearing, no matter how much they dislike it and no matter how certain they are that it is wrong. First, the majority should realize that they may be wrong, human judgment being inherently fallible, although people are far more willing to admit their fallibility in the abstract than in concrete cases. If the opinion turns out to be correct, they will have the opportunity to exchange error for truth and be the better for it. Even if the dissenting opinion is wrong, its articulation may spark a debate which allows the holders of the orthodox opinion to have a clearer perception and livelier impression of its truth, gained from witnessing its collision with error. "However unwilling a person who holds a strong opinion may be to admit that the opinion may be false, he ought to be moved by the consideration that, however true it may be, if it is not fully, frequently, and fearlessly discussed, it will be held as a dead dogma, not as a living truth."

Because he was a religious skeptic, it is not surprising that Mill refused to exempt the doctrines of the established church from this need for constant critical scrutiny, and indeed he used Christian doctrines as the sort of opinions that were often held as dead dogmas rather than living truths because they were rarely invigorated by encountering challenge. It is more to his lasting credit that he tried to hold science, whose claims many were beginning to accept uncritically, to a similar standard. "Even in natural philosophy [science]," he wrote, "there is always some other explanation possible on the same facts; some geocentric theory instead of heliocentric; some phlogiston instead of oxygen." Unless we know why one theory must be true and the other cannot be, we do not know the grounds for our opinion.

I give Mill credit for trying, but his examples would not shake the conviction of scientific triumphalists that while there may have been many false turns in the past, what science knows *now* it knows for sure. Now that Mill's doctrines have themselves become orthodox, there is a danger that many will hold them as dead dogmas, applicable to others but not to themselves. I wonder, though, why a utilitarian like Mill would expect or even desire that people be such disinterested truth-seekers. A settled opinion may be useful even if false, and that should be enough for a utilitarian.

Alexander Solzhenitsyn and the Freedom to Do Good

Another essay that could also have been titled "On Liberty" but which is entirely different from Mill's is Alexander Solzhenitsyn's speech at Harvard University's June 1978 commencement, later published as *A World Split Apart*. Before he gave this speech, Solzhenitsyn was much honored in the liberal media as a hero of the resistance to Soviet tyranny and was presumed to be a great admirer of Western liberal society. Although many people agreed with the criticisms of American society expressed in the speech, afterward Solzhenitsyn was widely dismissed in elite circles as a cranky religious eccentric who should not be taken seriously. Perhaps his greatest offense was telling his Harvard audience bluntly that "today's Western society has revealed the inequality between the freedom for good deeds and the freedom for evil deeds." By 1978 drawing a sharp distinction between good and evil seemed obsolete and illiberal to fashionable opinion. Twenty-four years later a similarly relativist fashion deplored President George W. Bush's reference to an "axis of evil."

Unfashionable also was Solzhenitsyn's claim that "it is time, in the West, to defend not so much human rights as human obligations." He continues:

> On the other hand, destructive and irresponsible freedom has been granted boundless space. Society has turned out to have scarce defense against the abyss of human decadence, for example against the misuse of liberty for moral violence against young people, such as motion pictures full of pornography, crime, and horror. This is all considered to be part of freedom and to be counterbalanced, in theory, by the young people's right not to look and not to accept. Life organized legalistically has thus shown its inability to defend itself against the corrosion of evil.

Solzhenitsyn's vision was more prophetic than backward-looking, as may be illustrated by one of his examples: "When a government earnestly seeks to root out terrorism, public opinion immediately accuses it of violating the terrorists' civil rights."

Solzhenitsyn attributed the "tilt of freedom toward evil" to a humanistic concept according to which man "does not bear any evil within himself, and all the defects of life are caused by misguided social systems, which must therefore be corrected." In short, he was attacking one of his audience's most deeply held prejudices, the assumption of a benevolent human nature.

In another passage from the lecture, Solzhenitsyn sounded more like Mill. He said:

> Without any censorship in the West, fashionable trends of thought and ideas are fastidiously separated from those that are not fashionable, and the latter, without ever being forbidden, have little chance of finding their way into periodicals or books or being heard in colleges. Your scholars are free in the legal sense, but they are hemmed in by the idols of the prevailing fad. There is no open violence, as in the East; however, a selection dictated by fashion and the need to accommodate mass standards frequently prevents the most independent-minded persons from contributing to public life and gives rise to dangerous herd instincts that block successful development.

In short, he warned his audience against the tyranny of the prevailing opinion.

The primary difference between Mill and Solzhenitsyn was that the former lived in a secure and confident nation with a powerful moral code that was sometimes oppressive. The latter knew only too well how liberal freedom is menaced from outside by totalitarian powers and from inside by unrestrained criminality. Which is the greater danger, that government will fail to root out terrorism or that it will violate the terrorists' civil rights? Mill wouldn't have understood the question, nor, I think, did Solzhenitsyn's 1978 audience. In 2002 we are at last beginning to understand. One society needs to reminded not to be overconfident and to make room for new ideas. Another society needs more to be exhorted to recover its courage and to remember some old truths. That is why our two spokesmen for liberty seem so different. They were

addressing very different situations. Grasp that and you may agree
that Solzhenitsyn was doing just what Mill praised. He was dissenting from the dead dogmas of 1978 liberalism and thereby providing his audience with an immense benefit, if they could only set
aside their prejudices and open their minds to some unfamiliar
wisdom.

The Right Questions About Truth and Liberty

**❶ Is there a sound religious or philosophical basis for liberal
freedom?**

As I was preparing this chapter I discovered a thought-provoking
article by Edward Skidelsky in the January 2002 issue of the British
left-liberal magazine *Prospect* (online at <www.prospect.com>).
The article was titled "A Liberal Tragedy," and its stated theme was
that "by cutting itself off from its Christian roots, liberalism has
become shrill and dogmatic, but there is no other way." Skidelsky
observed that liberalism originally derived its principles of equality,
liberty and toleration either from Christian tradition or from the
supposed attributes of human nature. Both of these sources have
had to be abandoned. "Human rights are held to be a universal possession, not the sole patrimony of Christians, yet those rights are
no longer grounded in belief in a universal human nature."

Skidelsky explained this last circumstance on grounds that will
be familiar to readers of the first chapter of this book. The classical
conception of man as a rational animal, separated by an unbridge-
able gulf from other animals, is condemned as "speciesism." The
dominant modern theory of human nature is purely biological; it

is concerned with those characteristics that we share with animals. The theory provides no basis for human rights. As we head into a brave new world of biotechnology and computer-controlled systems, this absence of any foundation for human rights ought to be a matter of grave concern. Skidelsky is appropriately pessimistic.

> Thus rights are no longer deduced, either theologically or philosophically. They are proclaimed. Fiat has replaced argument. Our faith in our own civilization is without rational foundation. This accounts for the shrill, dogmatic tone of modern liberalism. Classical liberalism, as exemplified by Tocqueville, Mill, and Isaiah Berlin, was discursive and philosophical. It tried to engage its opponents, to appeal to their reason and humanity. It could afford the luxury of argument, because it rested securely on an idea of human nature as benevolent and reasonable. Modern liberalism does not rest on any such conception. What is left is a set of legal claims, advanced in peremptory fashion, with no appeal to common reason. In the absence of any positive ideal to support it, the liberal proclamation of individual freedom looks increasingly like a mere license to selfishness.

It is not only Muslims who draw that conclusion; Alexander Solzhenitsyn said something similar.

Skidelsky considers and rejects the possibility that the breach between liberalism and Christianity was an unfortunate accident of history, in which case it might be repaired. No, he insists, the estrangement of liberalism from Christianity followed an inexorable logic. Christianity gave birth to liberalism through its doctrine that an individual's relation to God constitutes a primary identity in contrast to other, secondary identities. "There is no longer Jew or Greek, there is no longer slave or free, there is no longer male and female; for all of you are all one in Christ Jesus" (Gal 3:28). The great tree of liberal freedom and universal human rights grew from that root. If a tree abandons its root, how can it survive?

Skidelsky does not answer that question, but he does say that the tragic plight of liberalism today could not have been avoided, because "Christianity, to be true to itself, had to transcend itself." Christianity had to secularize itself (into liberalism) in obedience to its own fundamental principle of universality. Today this moral imperative has been joined by practical considerations. With non-Christian minorities living within their borders, Western states can hardly return to Christian confession. In a world divided by religious strife, only a secular form of liberalism can underpin international order.

Skidelsky follows his own logic to the bitter end, even though I assume he must hate the conclusion. Here is his final paragraph:

> Thus the fate of liberalism is—in the precise sense of the word—tragic. A tragic fate is one that proceeds not from external and accidental causes, but according to an inexorable internal logic. This is precisely the situation of liberalism. It must sever itself from its historic roots in Christianity, yet in doing so it severs itself from the source of its own life. Liberalism must follow a course that leads directly to its own atrophy. It must extirpate itself.

Skidelsky leaves Christians, and everybody else, with a very difficult question to answer. Is Christianity something universally valid, like reason or science, or is it merely one of many human religious belief systems, none of which could be valid for all times and places? In the latter case Christians may hope that their religion could live on under the protection of an international order underpinned by a secular form of liberalism, but Skidelsky explains that a purely secular liberalism is unlikely to survive for long because it would be severed from the source of its own life. In other words, Skidelsky's analysis greatly raises the stakes when we consider how important it is that Christian faith survive.

Previously it was possible to assume that if Christianity were to wither and die, a secular form of liberalism could survive indefinitely on a new foundation. If Skidelsky is right, the death of Christianity implies the withering of liberalism because there *is* no other foundation. To consider whether he may right, imagine that the international order will in the future be governed by the United Nations in cooperation with International Human Rights organizations, following the same principles that they now follow. Judging by how they have responded to the aftermath of the terrorist attacks of September 11, 2001, would you rely on these organizations, or an American government based on the same principles, to protect human rights and freedom under law? On the other hand, in a world divided by religious strife, is there an alternative?

If the tragic dilemma described by Skidelsky is real, then the fates of Christianity and liberalism are as linked as the fates of a tree and its root. I am not as pessimistic about this as Skidelsky because I believe that the original foundation is still living and available to be rediscovered. Liberal principles may persevere for a long time without any apparent foundation simply because they are attractive to most people. In that case insightful people will investigate the possibility that the original foundation remains sound after all, and perhaps it is the modernist biological view of human nature which ought to be discarded.

What is to be done about this situation? The immediate need is not to provide a solution but to frame the question in a way that permits us to find the solution if one exists. This is what I have tried to do in chapter eight.

EIGHT

The Ultimate Question

WHAT IS THE MOST IMPORTANT EVENT IN HUMAN HISTORY?

The Event Implies the Worldview

The answer you give to the ultimate question will imply an answer to the question I posed in an earlier chapter: What is the one correct religious worldview? Probably this question will confuse some readers who, like me, have been educated in naturalistic ways of thinking and may therefore imagine that I must be proposing a theocracy. On the contrary, I would oppose a theocracy of any kind, including a Christian theocracy, not in spite of the fact that I believe Christian theism to be the correct religious worldview, but *because* I believe the Christian teaching about the sinful heart of man. I know that theocrats wielding absolute power will not long remain Christians in any sense that I can recognize.

From Scripture I also know that when Pilate asked Jesus if he was the king of the Jews, Jesus answered that "my kingdom is not of this world." Muhammad, Lenin or any other worldly person would not have made that statement. A king or a president may be a Christian, and that he is a Christian should make a difference in what he says and does. This truism is a very long way from recommending a theocracy. Acceptance of religious pluralism—separation of church and state in American constitutional jargon—is one of the important ways in which Christianity differs from Islam, which contemplates an Islamic state, or from Marxist-Leninism, which implies what amounts to a materialist atheocracy (the dictatorship of the proletariat in communist jargon), which is every bit as rigid and coercive as any religious theocracy.

If you are shocked by the suggestion that there is *only one* correct religious worldview, that is probably because you have been indoctrinated to take naturalism/materialism for granted as "the way educated people think today," and so you are unaware that religious relativism is itself merely one way of thinking about religion and certainly *not* the position of all educated people. People are able to be relativists in one way only by being absolutist in some other way. For example, self-styled "skeptics" are generally dogmatic and authoritarian materialists. They are skeptical only toward things they dislike. A scientific atheist or a liberal agnostic is actually in agreement with a Christian like me, a Hindu pantheist or a Muslim in believing that there is only one correct religious worldview. The difference is over which of the mutually exclusive possibilities is correct. Christianity, Islam, Hinduism and scientific naturalism cannot all be correct unless the meaning of each possibility is so attenuated that it affirms very little. Whether a specific religious worldview is correct is one question. Whether and to what extent anyone would use force to ensure that his own religious worldview predominates over the others is a separate question. Almost anyone will approve of the use of force to protect his own creed and people from being dominated by murderous oppressors.

Perhaps Gandhi truly condemned violence in all circumstances, even to prevent a Hitler or an Osama bin Laden from ruling the world, but we may be certain that Gandhi's many Hindu and Christian admirers would not follow him to that extreme and would even kill him (as a Hindu actually did) if they thought such violence necessary to protect themselves from Islamist domination. I remember the beautiful movie *Gandhi,* which showed Gandhi's offer to turn the entire government of India over to the Muslims in a desperate effort to avert the violent Hindu-Muslim divorce that accompanied Indian independence. Assuming Gandhi truly meant that offer and had sufficient authority to make Hindus afraid that Muslim domination of all India was a real possibility, can you condemn that Hindu assassin without reservation?

Gandhi is acclaimed as one of the greatest saints of the twentieth century, but I wonder how he will look to the twenty-second century if India and Pakistan fight a nuclear war in the present century. There is a small measure of truth in the moral relativist's adage that "one man's terrorist is another man's freedom fighter." Lenin differed from Lincoln not in his willingness to employ violence but in the enthusiasm with which he did so and the ends that he sought to achieve. Those who think that any choice of ultimate purposes is arbitrary may see little difference between the two. One man kills thousands to end slavery, another kills millions to *impose* slavery, or just because he enjoys killing and wants the world to think him important. To a relativist who does not believe in any universal truth, or to a pacifist whose entire morality is limited to condemning violence, the difference is just a matter of subjective preference. Each to his own taste.

Now back to the ultimate question. What *is* the most important event in recorded history? I will suggest four possible answers. Anyone is free to propose others, but I predict that none of the others will survive for long in the glare of public scrutiny. The only criteria for eligibility, however, are that the event must be in recorded history (the invention of writing or the wheel does not qualify), and it must be important for everyone, not merely for members of a particular tribe or nation, or persons with some particular mission in life that other people do not necessarily share. For example, the speed of light in a vacuum is a specific figure and no other. This scientific fact, important for physicists, is true for everyone regardless of creed or nation, but no one would argue that it is the most important piece of knowledge for everybody to have. The most important event in history must be true in the relevant sense, and it also must be very important for everyone. Does any single event qualify?

The Incarnation

Christians should be able to give a confident answer to the ultimate question on the premise that the Gospels, summarized in the introductory verses of the Gospel of John, tell the truth. The incarnation and resurrection of Jesus Christ, the Word that became flesh and dwelt among us, is undoubtedly the most important event in the history of mankind if it actually happened as the Bible says. One may not know all sorts of things and be none the worse for it, but if God really lived on earth as a man and said and did the things that the Gospels report, then not to know these sayings and deeds, or to disregard them, is to be missing the one key that is capable of unlocking everything else. That is why it is of supreme importance that the good news must be made available to everyone, whether or not they choose to believe it.

The most devastatingly negative judgment must be made of any educational system which insists, as the schools of most nations do now, that students should not be taught the information they need to give an informed answer to the question posed by Jesus: "Who do you say that I am?" I am *not* saying that the schools must provide an answer to that question, much less endeavor to indoctrinate students in any "religious beliefs." What I *am* saying is that educators have a duty to ensure that students know what the Christian answer to the ultimate question is, and that they know what they need to know to understand why the question is important and to evaluate the answer. Specifically everyone should know the words and deeds of Jesus as recorded in the four Gospels. (Whether Jesus actually did and said these things is part of the question. That some semiliterate Galilean fishermen made the story up is another possibility, and Gospel critics are welcome to propose it or any other for consideration.)

We need not assume for this purpose that the Gospels are true, but it is grossly irresponsible to assume that they are so obviously false that they do not need to be mentioned. If the schools in North America, Europe, China, India, Israel and the Muslim nations would merely do as I am recommending here, that would be sufficient for my purpose. That the nations all fear to provide this basic education is itself an implicit answer to the underlying question. Given the opportunity, most people will be eager to learn the truth about the most important event in history. Because the Word is not merely a concept invented by men but a person able and willing to speak to sincerely inquiring minds and hearts, they will probably find the answer they seek. That is the terrifying possibility that motivates the nations in their educational systems to conceal the contents and even the existence of the Gospels. What they fear is not that the Gospels are false but that they might be true, or at least persuasive.

Receipt of the Qur'an

Muslims can also give a confident answer to the ultimate question. For them the most important event in history is Muhammad's receipt of the Qur'an directly from the one true God, together with Muhammad's proclamation of the Qur'an to the world and his consequent formation of the original Islamic society, supposedly an ideal state which modern Islamists aspire to revive. Muslims actually date their calendars from the year in which Muhammad made his migration, or *Hijira,* from Mecca to Medina, the turning point of his career.

The Qur'anic truth is universal if it is true at all because non-Muslims need to know Allah's wishes so they can submit to them in order to escape the wrath of Allah after death and the wrath of Allah's followers here on earth. The Islamic state has no place for those who do not submit to the will of Allah as revealed in the Qur'an, which explains the oppressive and sometimes violent mistreatment of unbelievers. Christianity as such does not have the same ambition to impose a theocracy, although some Christians have mistakenly thought so, usually with disastrous results. Most Christians are content to live in a secular state, provided the state grants them freedom to practice and proclaim their religion. This explains why the thoroughly Christian (Protestant) American society of the nineteenth century welcomed millions of Catholic and Jewish immigrants. It is inconceivable that an Islamic state or a Jewish state like modern Israel would do anything similar. American Christians do not feel threatened by non-Christian immigrants unless the new arrivals aspire to establish an anti-Christian state on whatever basis—materialist, Islamic or otherwise.

I cannot speak for all Christians, but I can say at least for myself that all students should also learn enough about the words and deeds of Muhammad to make an informed judgment about the credibility of Islam's claims, particularly in comparison to the claims of the Gospels concerning Jesus. I have no fear of the consequences, provided both cases are portrayed as fairly and completely as the circumstances allow, by accurate reporters rather than by spin doctors seeking to present only a prettified or demonized picture. This is a specific example of the general "teach the controversy" approach that led to the Santorum Amendment discussed in chapter one. Educators must make a judgment as to which controversies are sufficiently "alive" that they need to be taught. When educators use their authority in a biased or irresponsible way, as I allege scientific naturalists to have done, then the judgments of the educators must be reviewed in the legal and governmental process.

For many decades American educators have assumed that all topics they can classify as "religion" are sufficiently irrelevant to modern life that it is unnecessary or even harmful to include them in a curriculum. American educators in the 1970s may have thought it important that students learn something about communism because communism at the time was a serious contender for world domination. They would have thought it essential that students learn about biological evolution because that is "science," but they generally thought it unimportant for students to learn about Jesus, Muhammad or the Bible. We should expect that these priorities will change over time, and I believe that they are changing now. Lenin and Freud are in the dustbin of history, whereas the followers of Muhammad and Jesus are becoming more active in the world. The curriculum at all levels of education will have to reflect these trends if educators aspire to teach the young what they need to know.

Modern Science

Scientific naturalists have been telling the world for many years that the most important event in history was the discovery of modern science by geniuses such as Galileo, Newton and Darwin. Richard Dawkins has put this point of view nicely. If advanced extraterrestrials ever visit the earth, he wrote, the first question they will ask about us will be "Have they found out about evolution yet?" Scientific naturalists like Dawkins believe that science frees us from the superstition they associate with religion and thus gives mankind a prospect of peace, material abundance and health in a world governed by reason.

For the most visionary devotees of science, science even provides a promise of indefinitely prolonged life as we learn to download our mental "software" into computers/spaceships and then explore the universe at leisure. A generation or two from now, these futuristic visions may seem either prescient or absurd, depending on whether the technological wonders appear as predicted. We may say the same for the fantasies of human improvement that have been spun from the hype accompanying the Human Genome Project. If the geneticists finally make good on their promises, they will look very brilliant indeed, and scoffers like me will be forgotten in the resulting jubilation. Our great-grandchildren will have a much better view of the outcome than we can have now. Perhaps the fulfillment of the promises of genetic mastery will have given birth to a new era of human freedom or tyranny, or perhaps the great genome project will be remembered only as a very expensive delusion.

The American Republic

Some Americans and admirers of America may answer the ultimate question by saying that the most important event in history was the establishment of the American republic, with its constitutional guarantee of equal justice under law. In the words of Lincoln's Gettysburg Address, the United States of America was "a new nation, conceived in liberty and dedicated to the proposition that all men are created equal." I do not think that this American alternative is a satisfactory answer to the ultimate question, but to propose it for consideration is not as chauvinistic as it may seem. The premise is not that American society is inherently superior to

others, that its basic ideals are without antecedents or that its constitutional order (unlike the ideal Islamic state of legend) was not
grievously flawed from the outset. Of course, the practice of slavery contradicted the principle that "all men are created equal,"
and thus the seeds of the Civil War (and even women's suffrage)
were present from the beginning, long before the slave owners
realized what their agreement to the Constitution implied.

Democracy and equality existed as ideals even in the ancient
world, but they were associated with mob rule and lawlessness, as
in the French Revolution. Some American political ideas and institutions were borrowed from Britain, but nonetheless the American
republic was a *novus ordo seclorum* ("new world order"), to quote
the motto we put on the money. It is not the invention of liberty
and equality but the combination of these values with the rule of
law inherited from Britain that was America's gift to the world, and
this achievement qualifies the American example, notwithstand-
ing our grievous faults, to be considered of prime importance for
the entire world. The millions of immigrants who have come and
still come to America seeking freedom and opportunity provide
undeniable testimony to the universal appeal of the American
dream. Even Islamist terrorists yearn to come to America, if only
to take advantage of our freedoms to learn how to pilot hijacked
airliners, one of innumerable opportunities they would never be
offered in any Islamic country.

There are also some right questions to ask about the four proposed answers to the ultimate question. Each answer implies a
religious worldview, and the choice of worldview has important
consequences for government and society. An Islamic worldview

implies an Islamic society. A Christian worldview implies a different kind of society, not a theocracy but certainly a society in which Christians feel comfortable. I would argue that something has gone wrong with societies governed by any of the worldviews. In each case, what went wrong and why? My task in this book is to ask the questions rather than to answer them, but the job of asking is not complete unless the questioner provides some idea of what an answer may look like. To that end I will propose an hypothesis in each case—a tentative answer around which to organize further discussion and debate. If anyone can propose a better answer, I want to consider it.

Soviet Communism: What Went Wrong?

For practice I will start by analyzing a discarded answer to the ultimate question, one that would have been a serious contender not many years ago. The Communist Revolution of 1917-1918 gave the world the Soviet Union and similar dictatorships, which were for a long time admired in many countries, especially by intellectuals eager to try out bold social experiments as the inevitable wave of the future. We know now that just about everything went wrong with the communist experiment. Why was that? Can we attribute the failure to bad people who perverted a good idea, or was the idea bad from the outset?

I put this example first because the question is easy to answer, and it illustrates the general point I am making with all the other examples. Very few people outside of the most elite universities are so protected from reality that they can believe in Marxism today, but only a few decades ago many learned people would have said that the founding of the Soviet state was the most promising event in world history. It is not that communism made a wrong turn somewhere after getting off to a good start. Stalin, Mao and Castro did not betray the ideals of Lenin. Rather the evils that were implicit in Marxist-Leninist principles from the beginning came into full flower as the communist system became entrenched in power and able to override with force every faint remnant of better ideas and every scruple of conscience. No doubt Lenin and Stalin were evil men, but it is not very informative to stop with that observation. The more important question is why these evil men were able to amass so much power and do so much damage. I offer the hypothesis that the underlying defect in Marxist theory was that it contained no provision for sin, which is the inherent corruptibility of human nature. This tendency is likely to be especially dangerous in government leaders who rely on a theory they believe to be infallible. Communist theory did not provide a remedy for the likelihood that communist leaders would abuse whatever power they held. The founders of the American republic, whose understanding of human nature was Christian even if they were deists, provided an elaborate system of checks and balances because they recognized human nature's ability to be corrupted, a factor which the Marxists neglected.

Islam: What Went Wrong?

That question is usually asked these days in the context of the World Trade Center attack of September 2001, although it is better to ask what responsibility Islam bears for the fact that Muslim states are consistently ruled by corrupt and brutal tyrannies. Given this record of failure, it is questionable whether nations like Iraq, Syria and Egypt could ever become secular democracies where women are treated decently unless they first abandon Islam or change it drastically. In the aftermath of the attack national political leaders, understandably determined not to spark a worldwide religious conflict, reassured their citizens that the war on terrorism was not a war on Islam and that Islam was a religion of peace which was not responsible for terrorism. In some cases the reassurances were so enthusiastic that an unwary listener might have gained the impression that Muhammad had delivered the Sermon on the Mount, or at least had emphatically endorsed its teaching. More wary listeners pointed out that the terrorists themselves gave their lives in the belief that they were acting pursuant to authentic Muslim teaching, and that multitudes of cheering Muslims appeared to agree with them.

Even the supposedly "moderate" Muslim governments that the Western governments had relied on to keep the radicals in check turned out to be a great disappointment. Repeatedly Americans witnessed a seemingly responsible Muslim public figure, who had worked with apparent sincerity for good ecumenical relations while living in America, return to the Middle East and there deliver on state-sponsored media an anti-Jewish and anti-American tirade so crude that it would have embarrassed a Nazi propagandist. The "moderate" governments turned out to be subsidizing the radicals they were supposedly controlling, apparently in the hope that they would take their terrorism to Israel or America rather than practice it at home.

Even after all this was revealed, some influential journalists

continued to proceed on the apparent premise that Muslims are
the innocent victims of American imperialism or chauvinism, and
that the great evil to be feared was not Muslim terrorism but rather
discrimination against Muslims. This is not surprising; I remember well how many liberals thought (and still think) that the great
threat to liberty in the 1950s was not Stalinism but McCarthyism.
Were these journalists, and the academics and politicians who
agreed with them, perceptive or deluded?

I could answer that question but, in keeping with the purpose
of this book, I prefer to say only that what I have described is a
classic case of proclaiming the answer to a question that has never
been properly asked. It is not for relatively uninformed statesmen
like President George W. Bush or Prime Minister Tony Blair to tell
the world how Qur'anic teaching should be interpreted. That is a
task for the most influential Muslim leaders, and of course their
deeds speak far more eloquently than mere words. I see no evidence that Muslim leaders are eager to provide a candid answer to
my question about what went wrong, so if we wish to receive anything more informative than soothing platitudes, we must formu-
late the question precisely and press it very insistently. Muslim
leaders disavowing terrorism are a great deal like Darwinists
equivocating about scientific spokesmen for atheism. They generally want to distance themselves from terrorism without saying
anything that may seriously anger the terrorists.

To help frame a specific question, I propose this hypothesis: the
Islamist terrorists are correct that they are not perverting the
Qur'anic program but trying to fulfill it. Muslim leaders, especially
in the Middle East, may prevaricate to avoid the consequences of

affirming my hypothesis, but they will not deny it in words and deeds that make their denial credible to those who are less than overeager for reassurance that we can all just get along. Muslims are not taught to be at peace with unbelievers but to struggle relentlessly to bring them under Qur'anic rule. Just as the communists sometimes followed a policy of peaceful coexistence when it seemed convenient, Muslim aggression may be more apparent at some times than at others, but the underlying struggle is unrelenting.

Moreover, dedicated Muslims are not pragmatists, a fact that is difficult for most Americans to believe. America is the home of pragmatism, and the characteristic delusion of liberals is to believe even against all the evidence that other people, including totalitarians, are at heart very much like themselves. Franklin Delano Roosevelt seems to have thought he could charm Stalin into a reasonable frame of mind, and Lyndon Johnson thought he could make a deal with Ho Chi Minh. Totalitarians are not at all like liberals, and we may find that Muslim leaders are even less likely to respond pragmatically to offers and incentives than were communist dictators. An act of *jihad* such as a suicide bombing in a crowded public place does not have to achieve some ultimate goal such as the destruction of Israel in order to please Allah. Murderous acts that pragmatists instinctively describe as "senseless" are perfectly logical if you understand how Muslims think when they really believe the Qur'an. You may think my hypothesis true or false, but in either case it is more respectful of Muslims than misdescribing them as similar to Presbyterians whose peaceful intentions have been misunderstood.

If my hypothesis is to be evaluated in the context of a specific example, the best example would be the predicament of Palestinian Muslims under Israeli rule. The Palestinians, both Muslim and Christian, have genuine grievances that would attract powerful support in Europe, America and even Israel if the case were properly presented. In fact, they do attract considerable support, even though the case is never properly presented. Designing a successful strategy for the Palestinians would be easy. All the Muslims would have to do is to make common cause with the few remaining Christians, promise a secular Palestinian state with a constitution providing for equal justice under law, and then employ the protest methods that worked so well for Gandhi and Martin Luther King Jr. These methods would assuredly work just as well against Israel because the Israelis are a civilized people with a strong moral tradition derived from the Bible, and because Israel is dependent on the support of foreign governments that would dearly love to see the conflict settled. Instead the Palestinian Muslims murder civilians, including women and children, and give the impression that they will be satisfied by nothing less than the destruction of the Jewish state and the consequent massacre of its citizens.

Much as Americans might wish to walk away from this conflict, we cannot take responsibility for permitting another holocaust. Why don't the Palestinian Muslims pursue a strategy that may lead to success? That question is easy to answer on the premise that what they really want is to establish an Islamic state in Palestine, not a secular state. Making an alliance with Christians may bring short-term advantages, but it would undermine their real objective and be contrary to the revealed will of God. If a Muslim wishes to enter paradise, the best way of doing that is to die in a *jihad* rather than to bargain with infidels. From a Qur'anic standpoint Western pragmatists and liberals just don't understand what life is really about.

For purposes of comparison I want also to present an hypothesis contrary to my own. A Harvard professor of Islamic history, no Muslim himself, reportedly argued at a conference in late 2001 that Islamist radicalism is in retreat in modern Islam, which he said was becoming increasingly moderate and reformist.

> The Islamic learned men, he [the professor] said, have very limited interest in the political world. . . . "Better 60 years of oppression than one day of disorder," is a common sentiment among such leaders, representing their desire for spiritual accomplishment over worldly pursuits. (David Brooks, "Understanding Islam," *Weekly Standard*, January 21, 2002)

Very likely there are some such "leaders," but I wonder whom they are leading. Certainly not the crowds in the streets who cheer every terrorist act, nor the mothers who teach their sons to aspire to martyrdom in a *jihad*. I also wonder how the professor would explain the difference between the behavior of Palestinian Muslims and Palestinian Christians in the conflict over Israel. On the other hand, if we assume that my hypothesis is correct, then how could a distinguished professor of Islamic history be so out of touch with reality? I have an hypothesis for that also. For all his learning, the professor has been viewing Islam from the outside in, not living inside it and seeing the world from that perspective. There is a world of difference, and I know about it from my own experience as one who formerly viewed Christianity from outside and now views the world from inside Christianity. Perhaps Harvard would benefit if it included people with that kind of experience; I call that diversity.

For a much more realistic analysis of what has gone wrong with Islam, which still misses the point, see the article on this subject by Bernard Lewis in the January 2002 *Atlantic Monthly*. Lewis concedes that all Islamic countries are in a deplorable condition today, but he acquits Islam itself of responsibility for the decline because Islamic culture was so much more progressive many centuries ago. Lewis concludes, "To a Western observer, schooled in the theory and practice of Western freedom, it is precisely the lack of freedom—freedom of the mind from constraint and indoctrination, to question and inquire and speak; freedom of the economy from corrupt and pervasive mismanagement; freedom of women from male oppression; freedom of citizens from tyranny—that underlies so many of the troubles of the Muslim world. But the road to democracy . . . is long and hard, full of pitfalls and obstacles." What requires explanation is why Christian countries overcame these obstacles and Muslim countries uniformly did not. What was the difference, other than the Islamic mindset?

Christianity: What Went Wrong?

The Christian faith is in decay primarily in its home countries of Europe and North America, and this may give people the false impression that the situation is much the same everywhere else. On the contrary, a vibrant faith community is growing up in Africa and Asia, and this is not the work primarily of foreign missionaries but of courageous local people whose faith has been refined in the fires of persecution. The majority of faithful Christians now live in what we used to call the Third World. Persecution is particularly fierce in Muslim and Hindu countries because the ruling groups there fear that the gospel will be powerfully attractive to their oppressed people if they are allowed to hear it. Why do you think that the Taliban rulers, for example, felt so threatened by a few relief workers who brought Bibles with them?

If we consider the whole world, the Christian faith is still very attractive. Koreans and Africans are even considering sending missionaries to America to rekindle the dying embers of faith in our mainline denominations, and I hope they do. I like to tell Christian audiences that our faith thrives in the long run when we are persecuted, painful as that may be for those who have to endure it. What Christianity can't stand is wealth and respectability. This factor explains why the established churches of Europe in particular have so badly decayed. They became part of the government and, worse, of the social establishment. I could say only half-jokingly that a church which joins a social establishment puts itself in bondage to the second law of thermodynamics, the principle that every complex thing breaks down unless strenuous efforts are constantly made to renew it. In Europe Christianity is associated with mindless conformity, hypocrisy, and social privilege. In China it is associated with freedom from atheistic totalitarianism. What more do you need to know?

American Culture: What Went Wrong?

The notorious American Taliban soldier mentioned in chapter five

and the transgendered son of chapter six are not freaks but color-
ful examples of the logical consequences of underlying ideas that
are enthusiastically approved in American educational circles.
These are, specifically, the absolutizing of the racialist or multiculturalist version of "diversity" and the delusion that the difference
between boys and girls is merely a matter of socially constructed
"gender," which can be altered or abolished at will.

To provide a more complete picture of what has gone wrong in
America, I should add an example from the business culture. In
late 2001 Americans were shocked by the largest corporate bank-
ruptcy ever when the opulent and influential Enron Corporation
was suddenly revealed to be a hollow shell with massive debts and
losses concealed by accounting tricks. Even more shocking to me
was the involvement in the scandal of the public accounting profession through the leading firm of Arthur Andersen & Company.
Was this debacle the fault of a few corrupt individuals, or did it
point to underlying flaws in the culture of American business? Of
course there *were* some corrupt individuals, as there always are.
The pertinent question (as with Lenin) is why they were able to go
so far before being exposed, so that their eventual downfall caused
such enormous financial damage.

My father was a partner in Arthur Andersen until his death in
1966, so I felt a personal identification with that long-respected
firm's undoing. I remember as a child hearing my dad talk about
the accounting business and how important it was for accounting
firms to avoid any extraneous business involvement with clients
that might compromise their objectivity when evaluating the cli-
ent firm's financial statements. Why was that elementary principle

ignored not only by Arthur Andersen & Company but by other prestigious accounting firms? In the 1930s such a moral failure in business would have been blamed reflexively on capitalism, with reformers calling for government to take over the companies and replace management with salaried civil servants. Experience has since taught all those who are willing to learn from it that direct government management is not a cure for the evils of competitive free enterprise but a way of making those evils still more intractable by removing the discipline of the market.

But if it is simplistic to blame capitalism, then what *was* to blame? My hypothetical answer to that question ties together all the examples of recent American failures. What went wrong was that Americans in the mid-twentieth century abandoned the complex religious understanding that had served the nation well until that time. Before about 1960, American culture kept two distinct religious strains in creative tension with each other. One was the deist/rationalist strain derived from Thomas Jefferson and European intellectuals, and the other was the evangelical Christian strain stemming from the British evangelists John and Charles Wesley, George Whitefield, and their many American followers. Alexis de Toqueville's *Democracy in America* eloquently describes how essential the religious element was in forming the traits of character required for a successful encounter with the challenges posed by an unprecedented level of personal freedom. America gained much from the mixture of personal piety with a secular rationalism that kept the piety from reaching suffocating levels.

After the cultural triumph of Darwinism, however, the rationalists became dogmatic scientific materialists and set about driving the Christians to the margins of society, denying them influence in government, education or cultural life. The Christians bear as much responsibility for this situation as the rationalists because they gave up their position almost without a struggle. Because science provides no basis for value judgments, the culture accordingly turned to legalism as the only means of controlling behavior, and to relativistic background philosophies that made all rules and standards appear to be arbitrary exercises of power. The prime failure was one of cognition, and so the greatest damage was done in the elite universities and in the professions influenced by those universities.

The influence of a crucial element in the cultural mixture was greatly diminished, so that even inherently good things were allowed to become overbalanced and hence destructive. Science is a good thing, but not when it aspires to rule over religion and philosophy. Free economic enterprise is a good thing, but not when earning ever larger piles of money becomes the prime purpose of life. Even the infamous tyranny of political correctness started out as a good thing. It is good to avoid hurting the feelings of vulnerable people, even if you think the "victims" are unduly sensitive. When the victims become so powerful that they can suppress every word and idea they don't like, however (the paradox of powerful victims is paradoxical no longer), then a corrective is badly overdue. I believe that this corrective process is already under way, and I hope that this book helps to explain how and why it has begun.

Science: What Went Wrong?

What went wrong in science is that influential scientists became so devoted to ideological causes, including those that expanded the power and prestige of science, that they neglected their primary duty to test all theories impartially, including those from which they derive wealth and prestige. In biomedical science especially, many scientists were no longer content to live on comfortable salaries but aspired to own substantial interests in biotechnology companies. By the year 2000 editors of scientific journals were seriously concerned about undisclosed financial conflicts of interest on the part of authors who were posing as impartial scientific evaluators. Some scientists had placed themselves in a position akin to that of the accounting firms just before the Enron debacle. I refrain from saying more because I believe that events will eventually make the necessary points for me.

Above all, what went wrong in the developed countries where science predominates was that the prevailing culture, through its opinion-makers, gave up on the search for truth. They sorted all thoughts into two baskets, "religion" and "science." Then they kept everything in the "science" basket, however contrary to the evidence, and threw out everything in the "religion" basket, however often it had been confirmed by experience. That left the most technologically advanced societies with a definition of knowledge that allowed knowledge only of means and relegated all questions of ultimate ends to the realm of subjectivity and speculation. Like a traveler without a map or a compass, these societies no longer had any knowledge of where they should be going. Not surprisingly, they lost their way.